# LERNPLUS+

DIE LERNHILFE FÜRS GYMNASIUM

## ENGLISCH
## 9./10. SCHULJAHR

Schroedel

LERNPLUS⁺
**Englisch 9./10. Schuljahr**

Autoren:
**Bernd Raczkowsky** unterrichtet Englisch an einem Gymnasium in Augsburg und ist seit mehr als 30 Jahren im Schuldienst tätig. Er war Fachbetreuer für Englisch, leitet studienbegleitende Seminare an der Universität Augsburg und ist Mitarbeiter der Schulleitung.
**Christof Wagner** hat langjährige Unterrichtserfahrung als Gymnasiallehrer in Bayern. Auch er ist in der studienbegleitenden Seminarausbildung und als Fachbetreuer für das Fach Englisch tätig.



Druck [2] / Jahr 2015

Herstellung: Dirk von Lüderitz
Umschlaggestaltung und Layout: Janssen Kahlert Design & Kommunikation GmbH, Hannover
Umschlagfoto: Fotosearch
Illustrationen: Jan Bintakies, Hannover
Redaktion und Satz: imprint, Zusmarshausen
Druck und Bindung: westermann druck GmbH, Braunschweig

ISBN 978-3-507-**23165**-8

**Liebe Schülerin, lieber Schüler,**

Lernplus hilft dir, die wichtigsten Inhalte des Englischunterrichts in der Jahrgangsstufe 9 und 10 zu wiederholen, zu üben und besonders die Themen zu trainieren, die erfahrungsgemäß viele Stolpersteine enthalten. Mit Lernplus kannst du deine Wissenslücken schließen. Alle Kapitel sind überschaubar gegliedert und alle Regeln werden Schritt für Schritt erklärt, bevor du sie in den Übungen selbstständig anwendest.

**Training plus** fragt dein Wissen am Ende eines Kapitels noch einmal ab. Mithilfe der insgesamt 99 Testfragen kannst du gut überprüfen, wie sicher du die einzelnen Regeln beherrschst.

Den **Abschlusstest** nach jedem Kapitel bearbeitest du so wie eine Klassenarbeit. In der Regel gibt es für jede Teilaufgabe einen Punkt, bei schwierigeren Aufgaben zwei Punkte. In den Lösungen findest du eine Punkteübersicht, mit der du deine Leistungen einschätzen kannst.

In Lernplus gibt es außerdem drei besondere Elemente:

**Regel** Die Regeln werden in jedem Kapitel verständlich zusammengefasst und anschaulich erklärt. Oft werden sie durch Beispiele ergänzt.

**Tipp** Hier findest du Hinweise, worauf du beim Lernen achten solltest oder wie du dir etwas besonders gut merken kannst.

**Info plus** Weißt du, warum der höchste Berg der Welt nach dem Briten Sir George Everest benannt ist? Und wie viel Grad Celsius herrschen, wenn der Wetterbericht von 86 Grad Fahrenheit spricht?
Für alle, die etwas mehr wissen wollen, bietet Info plus spannende Informationen oder Hintergründe – etwa zur Landeskunde.

Mithilfe der **Lösungen** im Anhang kannst du kontrollieren, ob du die Aufgaben richtig bearbeitet hast und wie viele Punkte du im Abschlusstest erzielt hast. Wenn du im Buch nicht genügend Platz für die Bearbeitung der Übungen findest, schreibe die Lösungen bitte in ein Heft.

Viel Erfolg beim Üben und Besserwerden mit Lernplus wünscht dir

das **Lernplus-Team**

# 1 Zusammenschau der englischen *tenses*

**In den vergangenen Schuljahren wurden die *tenses*, also die Zeitformen im Englischen, eingeführt und ausgiebig geübt. Nun am Übergang zur Oberstufe ist es wichtig, diese *tenses* noch einmal in einer Synopse, also einer Zusammenschau, zu festigen.**

## 1.1 Bildung der *tenses*

Regel

Grundsätzlich gibt es im Englischen die gleichen **Zeitstufen** wie im Deutschen, also Gegenwart, Vergangenheit und Zukunft. Für jede dieser Zeitstufen existieren ***tenses***, also Formen, mit denen man diese Zeitstufen ausdrücken kann. Im Gegensatz zum Deutschen, wo die entsprechenden Formen (z.B. Imperfekt, Plusquamperfekt usw.) meist tatsächlich nur den zeitlichen Bezug beschreiben, **drücken die englischen *tenses* auch andere Bezüge** (z.B. ein Wollen, eine Absicht usw.) **aus.** Darüber hinaus gibt es für die englischen *tenses* auch noch zwei unterschiedliche **Aspekte** *(aspects)*, nämlich ***simple aspect*** und ***progressive aspect***. Der ***simple aspect*** bezieht sich auf Aktivitäten, die gewohnheitsgemäß immer wieder so verrichtet werden (z.B. *I go to school from Monday to Friday*), der ***progressive aspect*** auf solche, die **gerade** stattfinden, stattfanden oder stattfinden werden (z.B. *He's reading the newspaper. She was watching TV, when suddenly the doorbell rang. He will be holding the lesson on evolution next Monday.*).

**Übersicht: Bildung der *tenses***

Die ***simple present*-Form** des Verbs entspricht der Grundform des Verbs (***infinitive***): → *You know a lot about history*. In der dritten Person Singular wird an das Verb ein ***-s*** angehängt: → *She know**s** a lot about biology.*

Das ***present progressive*** wird mit der entsprechenden Form von ***be*** und der ***-ing*-Form** des Verbs gebildet: → *He **is** do**ing** his homework. **Are** you wait**ing** for your brother?*

Das ***simple past*** wird bei den regelmäßigen Verben dadurch gebildet, dass man an die Stammform des Verbs die Endung ***-ed*** anhängt: → *I walk**ed** a lot last week.* Liegen unregelmäßige Formen vor, so wird die zweite Verbform verwendet (z.B. *sing* – ***sang*** - *sung*): → *The band **sang** about twenty songs in the concert.*

Das ***past progressive*** wird mit einer Form von ***be*** (*was/were*) und der ***-ing*-Form** des Verbs gebildet: → *He **was** walk**ing** while they **were** talk**ing**.*

Das ***simple present perfect*** wird mit ***have*** bzw. ***has*** (3. Person Singular) und der ***past-participle*-Form *des Verbs*** gebildet. Bei den **regelmäßigen Verben** (*regular verbs*) entspricht diese Form der Stammform des Verbs mit angehängtem ***-ed:*** → *They **have** work**ed** so much so far this month*. Bei den **unregelmäßigen Verben** (*irregular verbs*) entspricht diese Form der dritten Form des gelernten Verbs: → *sing - sang - **sung*** → *She **has sung** so many songs for me.*

Das ***present perfect progressive*** bildet man mit ***have been*** bzw. ***has been*** und der ***-ing*-Form** des Verbs: → *She **has been** talk**ing** to her for ages.*

Das ***simple past perfect* wird mithilfe von *had*** und der ***past-participle*-Form** des Verbs (dritte Form) gebildet: → *We **had** walk**ed**. They **had caught** the thief.*

Das ***past perfect progressive*** wird in allen Personen mit ***had been*** und der ***-ing*-Form** des Verbs gebildet: → *They **had been** walk**ing.***

Das ***simple future*** *(future I)* wird mit ***will*** und der Infinitiv-Form des Verbs gebildet:
→ *Paul **will spend** his holidays in Spain next month.*

Das ***future progressive*** wird mit ***will*** plus ***be*** und der ***-ing*-Form des Verbs** gebildet:
→ *Our professor **will be** hold**ing** his seminar on ornithology next term.*

Das ***simple future perfect*** *(future II)* wird mit ***will*** plus ***have*** und der ***past-participle*-Form des Verbs** gebildet: → *On Monday in two weeks she **will have** talk**ed** about the story.*

Das ***future perfect progressive*** wird so gut wie nie verwendet. Zur Vollständigkeit hier die Formen: *My friend **will have been** carry**ing** the box home.* (also: ***will* + *have been* + *-ing*-Form** des Verbs)

Tipp

**Ein Satz in allen *tenses***

Man kann Sicherheit im Umgang mit den *tenses* erreichen, indem man sich einen einfachen Satz einprägt und diesen in allen möglichen *tenses* und *aspects* formuliert. Dies ist dann ein Grundgerüst für das Zusammenbauen komplexerer Sätze.

| | ***simple form*** | ***progressive form*** |
|---|---|---|
| ***present tense*** | *I work.* | *I am working.* |
| ***past tense*** | *I worked.* | *I was working.* |
| ***present perfect*** | *I have worked.* | *I have been working.* |
| ***past perfect*** | *I had worked.* | *I had been working.* |
| ***future*** | *I will work.* | *I will be working.* |
| ***future perfect*** | *I will have worked.* | *I will have been working.* |

**1** Bilde die entsprechenden Formen der Verben.

**simple present**

He ____________ … (go). They ____________ … (hide). It ____________ … (work).

She ____________ … (talk). They ____________ … (flee). I ____________ … (walk).

**present progressive**

You ________________________ … (try). She ________________________ … (do).

I ________________________ … (hold). He ________________________ … (run).

I ________________________ … (leave). You ________________________ … (sleep).

**simple past**

She ____________ … (jump). We ____________ … (kick). I ____________ … (give).

They ____________ … (create). He ____________ … (think). You ____________ …(bite).

**past progressive**

He ________________________ … (talk). They ________________________ … (put).

It ________________________ … (rain). She ________________________ … (go).

You ________________________ … (speak). I ________________________ … (think).

**simple present perfect**

He ________________________ …(try). They ________________________ …(hide).

I ________________________ … (send). We ________________________ … (change).

You ________________________ … (lose). She ________________________ … (throw).

**present perfect progressive**

She ________________________________________________ … (listen).

It ________________________________________________ … (run).

He ________________________________________________ … (say).

They ________________________________________________ … (teach).

We ________________________________________________ … (ring).

You ________________________________________________ … (show).

**simple past perfect**

He ____________________ … (leave). They ____________________ … (go).

She ____________________ … (kick). We ____________________ … (beat).

It ____________________ … (happen). They ____________________ … (sell).

**past perfect progressive**

They ________________________________________ … (watch).

He ________________________________________ … (sit).

You ________________________________________ … (drive).

We ________________________________________ … (hold).

Mary ________________________________________ … (swim).

I ________________________________________ … (work).

**simple future**

You ________________________________________ … (dive).

We ________________________________________ … (spend).

He ________________________________________ … (stay).

**future progressive**

I ________________________________________ … (set).

You ________________________________________ … (hide).

She ________________________________________ … (run).

Tipp

**Nicht vergessen: Endkonsonantenverdoppelung und stummes *-e***

Nach kurz gesprochenem Vokal wird der **Endkonsonant** verdoppelt:

*drop* ➞ *past tense: dro**pp**ed;* ➞ ***-ing*-Form:** *dro**pp**ing*

*sit* ➞ ***-ing*-Form:** *si**tt**ing; rub* ➞ *past tense: ru**bb**ed;* ➞ ***-ing*-Form:** *ru**bb**ing;*

Ein nicht gesprochenes *-e* (**stummes *-e***) fällt in der ***-ing*-Form** weg

*clos**e*** ➞ *closing*

*mak**e*** ➞ *making*

*leav**e*** ➞ *leaving*

## 1.2 Verwendung der *present tenses*

Regel

**Verwendung des *simple present* und des *present progressive***

Für alle Zeitachsen gilt:
V = Vergangenheit; MOS = *moment of speaking*; Z = Zukunft;

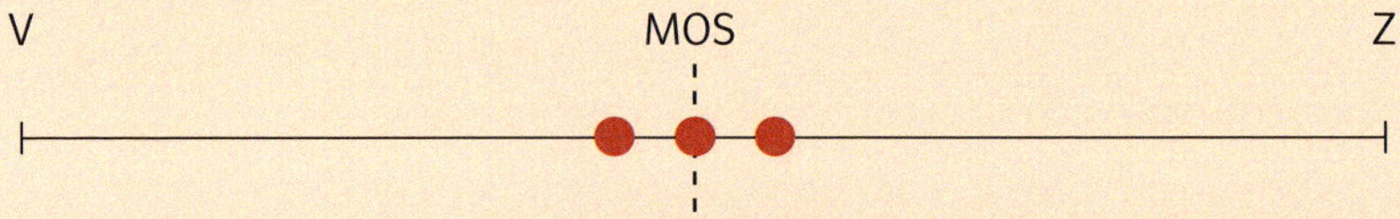


Das ***simple present*** wird für Zustände und Gewohnheiten verwendet, die immer wieder (also z.B. gestern, heute und in Zukunft) so stattfinden: *I go to school by bus.* Außerdem verwendet man diese *tense* auch für *universal truths* (allgemeine Wahrheiten): *The sun sets in the west.*

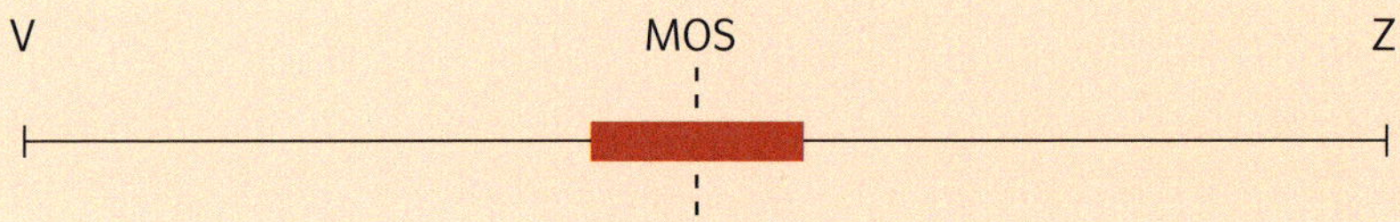


Das ***present progressive*** wird für Handlungen und Aktionen verwendet, die im Augenblick des Sprechens oder „zur Zeit" passieren: *He's living in New York at the moment. They're playing tennis.*

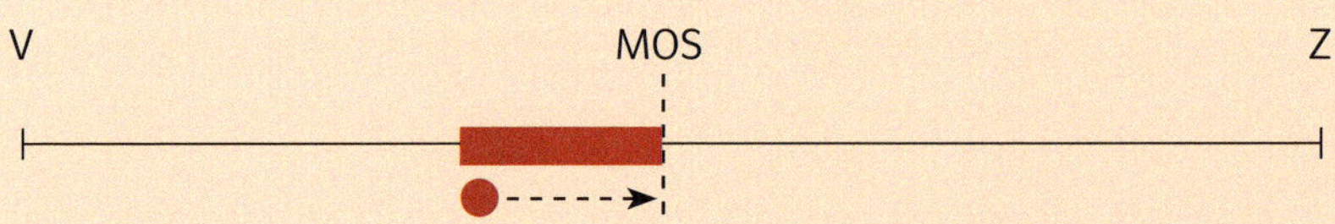


Das ***simple present perfect*** wird verwendet für Handlungen, die in der Vergangenheit angefangen haben und bis zum Zeitpunkt des Sprechens andauern *(up to now)* oder wo das Ergebnis der Handlung in der Gegenwart noch erkennbar ist (resultatives *present perfect*): *Where have you been? I've waited for you for three hours! - Sorry, I missed the bus and so I walked up here.*

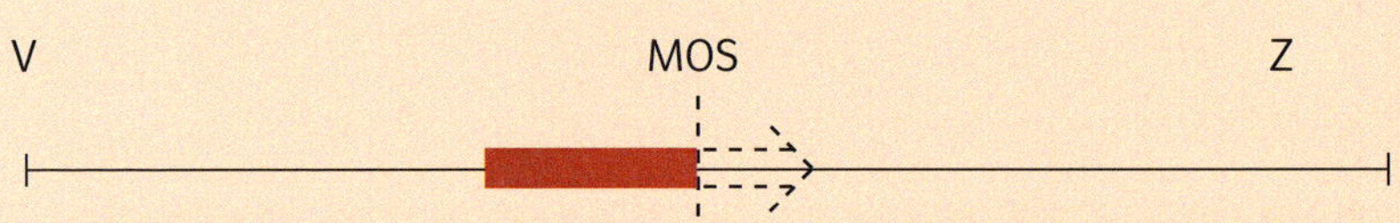


Das ***present perfect progressive*** wird verwendet, wenn in der Vergangenheit begonnene Handlungen/Aktionen bis in die Gegenwart und darüber hinaus andauern: *Where is Susan? - I don't know. I've been waiting for her since 9.*

## 2 Verwende die *present tenses* richtig.

a) Are you joking? - No, I ______________________ (tell) you the truth.

b) If you heat ice, it ______________________ (melt).

c) Oh, look, the streets are wet. It ______________________ (rain).

d) She ______________________ (work) as a physician for ten years now, but tomorrow she will start her new job in the hospital.

e) __________ you ever __________ (have) to Scotland? - No, I __________ .

f) __________ he __________ (post) the letter? - Not yet.

Tipp

**Zeitangaben der Vergangenheit und Signalwörter**

Sobald eine **Zeitangabe der Vergangenheit** wie etwa ***last year, in 1950*** oder auch nur ***two minutes ago*** in einem Satz vorkommen, wird das ***simple past tense***, nicht das ***present perfect*** verwendet.

Die Signalwörter ***since*** (*seit* einem Zeitpunkt) und ***for*** (*seit* Zeitspanne) verlangen eine Form des ***present perfect***.

Handlungen, die in der Vergangenheit angefangen haben, bis jetzt andauern und noch weitergehen, werden im Deutschen im Präsens ausgedrückt: Meine Mutter arbeitet seit 1995 als Pilotin. → *My mother has been working as a pilot since 1995.*

## 3 Übersetze.

a) Michel sitzt seit zwei Stunden im Schuppen *(shed)*.

______________________________________________

b) Er weiß nicht warum. ______________________

c) Aber sein Vater schickt ihn immer in den Schuppen, wenn er etwas angestellt hat.

______________________________________________

______________________________________________

d) Obwohl er immer versucht nett zu sein, hat er diese Woche schon fünfmal den Nachmittag im Schuppen verbracht.

______________________________________________

______________________________________________

e) Gerade schnitzt *(to carve)* er ein Holzmännchen *(wooden figure)*.

______________________________________________

f) Er tut das immer, wenn er im Schuppen ist.

______________________________________________

g) Diese Woche hat er schon fünf Männchen fertiggestellt.

______________________________________________

h) Das letzte sieht aus wie sein Lehrer.

______________________________________________

## 1.3 Verwendung der *past tenses*

Regel

**Verwendung des *simple past*, des *past progressive*, des *simple past perfect* und des *past perfect progressive***

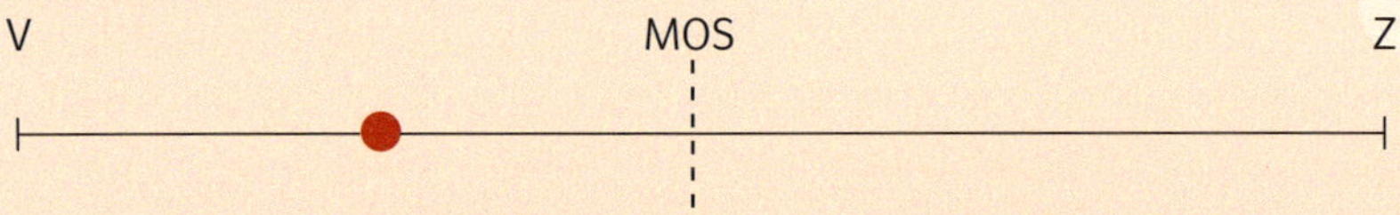


Für Handlungen, die in der Vergangenheit **abgeschlossen** wurden, verwendet man das ***simple past:*** → *She **went** to a Cold Play concert for the first time in 2007.*

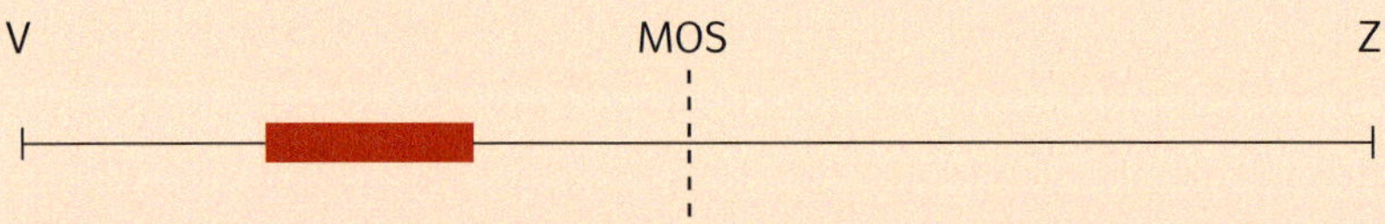


Handlungen, die zu einem bestimmten Zeitpunkt der Vergangenheit **gerade im Gange** waren (oft als Hintergrundhandlung), werden mit dem ***past progressive*** ausgedrückt: → *I **was sitting** in the bathtub when the phone started to ring.*

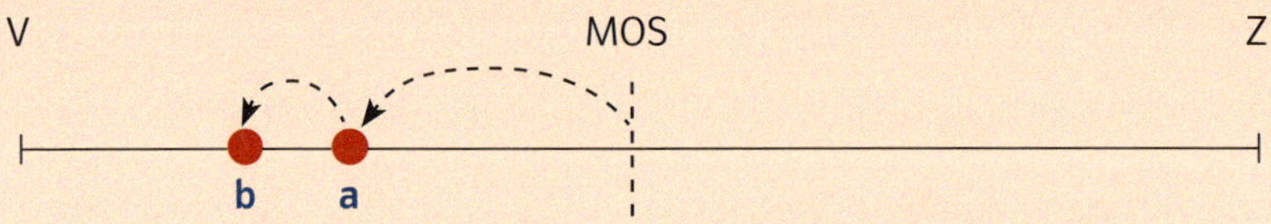


Handlungen, die **vor einer anderen Handlung in der Vergangenheit** ablaufen und abgeschlossen sind, werden mit dem ***simple past perfect*** ausgedrückt (Plusquamperfekt im Deutschen): → *Before he arrived* **(a)**, *he had decided* **(b)** *to stay overnight.*

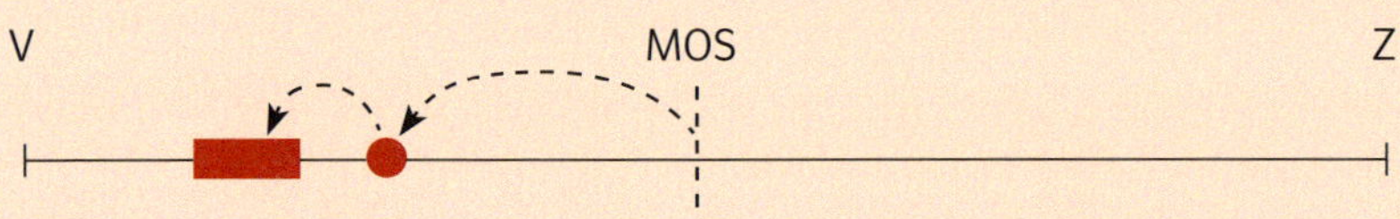


**Will man den *Verlauf* der weiter zurückliegenden Handlung betonen,** verwendet man das ***past perfect progressive:*** → *Before he arrived, he **had been walking** a long distance.*

**4** Finde im Text Beispiele für die einzelnen Zeiten und erkläre, warum sie an dieser Stelle verwendet werden. Schreibe in dein Heft.

Three months ago, Katy **started** to work as a waitress in a café. She **had** to work for 12 hours every weekend on Saturdays from 2 o'clock in the afternoon until 10 o'clock at night and on Sundays from 4 to 8. Her parents **were** not too happy about it, since she has her final exams this spring, but Katy simply **said**,"I **need** the money!". Normally the work **wasn't** too hard. The café **was** in a side street and there **were** not too many customers, especially on Saturdays.
Last weekend, however, everything **was** different. After she **had cleaned** the kitchen on Saturday, her boss **came** in. He **said**, "Susan won't be able to come tomorrow. She **has got** the flu. You **must** start earlier tomorrow and work till 10 o'clock!" Katy **did not** really **like** the idea of working so long the next day, but she **thought**, "I can use the money and especially the tips!"
When she **got to** the café at 2 o'clock, Rachel, the cook, **was waiting** for her. After they **had opened** up, the first customer **arrived** and then they **didn't have** any time to catch their breath until the café **was** empty at 9 o'clock. Rachel and Katy **had been cleaning** the mess in the kitchen for half an hour when a big, noisy group of young people **came** in and **ordered** some snacks. They **were laughing** and **having fun** until they **left** at 10.30, half an hour after closing time. When Katy **collected** the dirty plates and glasses, she **noticed** that they **had not** even **left** a tip.

**5** Setze die richtigen Vergangenheitsformen ein.

After Alan ________________ (leave) school, he ______________ (start) an apprenticeship at a bank. He ____________________________ (talk) to a customer one day, when a tall man __________________________ (come) in. The man ____________ (sort) nervously through some forms when Alan's phone ________________(ring). Alan ________________ (pick) it up and ______________(put) it down again after a voice ______________ (say), "Wrong number!" The man ____________________ (fill) in a form when he __________________ (drop) his pen and all the time Alan ________________ (wait) patiently. When he ______________ (turn) around to go back to the office the man _________________________ (come) to the counter. He _______________________ (want) to open a new account and _______________________ (hand) Alan a cheque for 100.000 $. Alan ___________________________ (begin to sweat) when he ______________________ (take) the cheque to the manager.

## 1.4 Verwendung der *future tenses*

Regel

**Möglichkeiten, die Zukunft auszudrücken**

Das Englische kennt mehrere Möglichkeiten, Zukünftiges auszudrücken.

1. Das ***will-future*** verwendet man, wenn man **sicher** ist, dass etwas passieren wird, was man **selbst nicht beeinflussen** kann, außerdem für **Vorhersagen und Annahmen**, aber auch für **Versprechen** und **spontane Entscheidungen**:
*My mother will send me to a boarding school, and I can't do anything about it.*
Es steht oft auch nach *I think, I hope, I expect, I'm afraid, I presume* und zusammen mit *surely* und *certainly: I hope she'll* ***be a star some day. – I'm sure she will.***

2. Mit dem ***going to-future*** drückt man aus, dass man etwas **vorhat (Intention, Plan)**:
*I 'm going to have a party for my birthday on Friday.*
Man verwendet es auch bei **Schlussfolgerungen**, also wenn konkrete Anzeichen für etwas, das gleich eintreten wird, vorhanden sind. *Look at the dark sky. It is going to rain soon.*

3. Das ***present progressive*** hat zukünftige Bedeutung, wenn eine private Übereinkunft (*private arrangement*) getroffen wurde: *We're having dinner in the new restaurant tonight.*

4. Das ***simple present*** kann Zukunft im Zusammenhang mit offiziellen Informationen (z.B. Fahrplan, Nachrichten) ausdrücken: *Our plane leaves at 10.45.*

5. Das ***will-future progressive*** drückt Zukunft aus, wenn erwartet wird, dass zu einem bestimmten Zeitpunkt in der Zukunft eine Handlung im Verlauf sein wird: *He will be sitting in the library for hours.*

6. Das ***future perfect*** entspricht dem **Futur II** im Deutschen, d.h. es drückt aus, dass eine **Handlung in der Zukunft abgeschlossen sein wird:** *They will have flown to Greece by this time next week.*

**6** Setze die richtigen Formen des Futur ein.

Anna ______________ (be) sixteen this summer. She ____________________ (have) a big party with all her friends and hopes they _______________ (give) her great presents. Her parents ____________________ (not, be) home as they ____________ _______________ (fly) to Greece for their summer holidays. Her friend Clara advised her, "Don't invite Lukas and his friends. They _______________ (drink) all night and then you ____________ ____________________(have to clean) your house for hours."

"When ____________________ (leave, your parents)?"

– "Their plane __________ (leave) two days before my birthday." – "Why ______

they ________ (go) away?" – "They __________ (meet) friends in Greece."

**Tipp** Im Deutschen steht oft das Präsens, wenn im Englischen das Futur (*will-future*) stehen muss: *She will do the job tomorrow.* → Sie erledigt die Arbeit morgen. In Adverbialsätzen mit *before, when, as soon as* und *until* steht nie *will* oder eine andere Form des Futurs.

## 7 Übersetze.

a) Nächste Woche treffe ich meine Brieffreundin aus Schottland.

______________________________

b) Ihr Flug kommt am Montag in Frankfurt an.

______________________________

c) Sie wird zuerst ein paar Tage bei ihrem Bruder in Würzburg verbringen.

______________________________

d) Ich hoffe, sie trinkt dort nicht zu viel Wein.

______________________________

e) Wenn sie zu mir kommt, wird sie sicherlich müde sein.

______________________________

f) Sobald ich 18 bin, nehme ich die ersten Fahrstunden.

______________________________

g) Mein Geburtstag ist im Mai, daher habe ich (dann) im Sommer die Prüfung bestanden.

______________________________

______________________________

h) Morgen werde ich einen Reiseführer über Schottland kaufen

______________________________

**1** Was bedeutet *simple*, was *progressive aspect* generell?

*simple*: ______________________________

______________________________

*progressive*: ______________________________

______________________________

**2** Warum ist das *present perfect* eigentlich keine reine Form der Vergangenheit?

______________________________

______________________________

**3** Worin besteht der Unterschied in der Verwendung von *simple past tense* und *simple present perfect*?

______________________________

______________________________

______________________________

**4** Welche *tenses* können beim Auftauchen der Signalwörter *since* und *for* verwendet werden?

______________________________

**5** Wann wird das *going to-future* verwendet? ______________________________

______________________________

______________________________

**6** Wann kann das *simple present* zum Ausdruck von Zukunft verwendet werden?

______________________________

______________________________

1 Vervollständige die Tabelle. ___/10

| | |
|---|---|
| **simple present** | |
| **present progressive** | |
| **simple past** | |
| **past progressive** | She was teaching her son Latin. |
| **simple present perfect** | |
| **present perfect progressive** | |
| **simple past perfect** | |
| **past perfect progressive** | |
| **simple will-future** | |
| **simple future perfect** | |
| **going to-future** | |

2 *simple past tense* oder *simple present perfect*? ___/5

My wife and I ____________________ (never, be) to Ireland. Last summer we ____________________ (decide) to go on holiday to France, although I ____________________ (be) to France about ten times already. But my wife ____________________ (not, agree). I ____________________ (not have) any chance to go to Scotland. It's always the same!

3 Übersetze. ___/9

a) Sir John hat (bisher) vierzehn Auszeichnungen erhalten. (eine Auszeichnung erhalten = *to be awarded a prize*) ____________________

____________________

b) Ich sah mir gerade einen Film von Steven Spielberg an, als da plötzlich ein lauter Knall war. ____________________

____________________

c) Gehst du morgen in die Schule? – Nein, ich bin seit vier Tagen krank.

____________________

____________________

**Gesamtpunktzahl ___/24**

# 2 *Passive voice:* das Passiv

**Das englische Passiv gilt bei vielen als ein grammatikalischer Stolperstein – ganz zu Unrecht, denn auch hier muss man ganz einfach systematisch vorgehen. Am besten lernt man anhand einfacher Sätzchen wie sie die folgende Tabelle zeigt.**

## 2.1 Verbformen im Passiv

Regel

**Überblick über die Verbformen im Passiv**

**Infinitive passive:** *be beaten; geschlagen/besiegt werden*

**Bildungsformel:** *be + past-participle*-Form des Verbs (also die dritte zu lernende Form des Verbs bei den unregelmäßigen Verben)

| ***simple aspect*** | ***progressive aspect*** |
|---|---|
| ***present tense*** | |
| *I'm beaten.*<br>*Ich werde besiegt.* | *He is being beaten.*<br>*Er wird gerade besiegt.* |
| ***past tense*** | |
| *She was beaten.*<br>*Sie wurde besiegt.* | *They were being beaten.*<br>*Sie wurden gerade besiegt.* |
| ***present perfect***<br>*He has been beaten.*<br>*Er wurde besiegt/ist besiegt worden.* | |
| ***past perfect***<br>*We had been beaten.*<br>*Wir waren besiegt worden.* | |
| ***will-future***<br>*She will be beaten.*<br>*Sie wird besiegt werden.* | |
| ***future perfect***<br>*You will have been beaten.*<br>*Du wirst besiegt worden sein.* | |

**1** Übertrage die Formen in das Passiv.

| active voice | passive voice |
|---|---|
| … pays … | *… is paid …* |
| … is leaving … | |
| … had known … | |
| … was checking … | |
| … washed … | |
| … knew … | |
| … will watch … | |
| … have beaten … | |
| … will have taken … | |
| … was going to fight … | |

## 2.2 Das Wesen des Passivs

Regel

**Das Passiv**

Das Passiv beschreibt, dass etwas mit jemandem getan wird, bzw. jemand etwas erleidet. Im Deutschen heißt diese Form deshalb die **Leideform** im Gegensatz zur Tatform (Aktiv). Das Passiv betont die Person oder die Sache, **mit der etwas passiert** und nicht die Person oder Sache, die eine Handlung ausführt. Entsprechend gebraucht man das Passiv (genauso wie im Deutschen) dann, **wenn der Teil, mit dem die Handlung geschieht**, also der passive und nicht der aktive Teil einer Handlung **für den Sprecher wichtig** ist.

Will man die aktive Person/Sache mit in den Passivsatz einbeziehen, muss man diese mit der Präposition ***by*** an den Passivsatz anschließen ***(by-agent)***. Er wird nur eingefügt, wenn die Information über den Täter wichtig erscheint:

→ *The cake was eaten **by** the dog.*

Das **direkte Objekt des Aktivsatzes** wird zum **Subjekt des Passivsatzes**, d.h. nur Verben, die ein direktes Objekt im Aktivsatz haben können (sogenannte transitive Verben), können ein Passiv bilden.

*Progressive forms* gibt es im Passiv nur im *present* und *past*.

**Modale Hilfsverben** bilden das Passiv mithilfe des ***passive infinitive***:

→ ***Handluggage** must be put **under the seat.***

**2** Setze die Aktivsätze ins Passiv um. Entscheide, wann du einen *by-agent* benötigst.

a) The sailors are loading the ship. ____________________

____________________

b) I will have told the story. ____________________

____________________

c) They had talked the problem over again and again. ____________________

____________________

d) She's going to finish her exam on Monday.____________________

____________________

e) Will they book the journey? ____________________

**3** Ergänze den Zeitungsbericht. Setze die Verben in die richtige Passivform um und fülle *by* ein, wo nötig.

Yesterday the theft of two valuable paintings ____________________ (dis-cover). They ____________________ (steal) from a flat in Bayswater. After the glass of a cellar door ____________________ (smash) the house ____________________ (enter) the bur-glars. Then the door to the study ____________________ (force) open and the pictures ____________________ (cut) from their frames __________ the burglars. As the owners of the flat are on holiday in the South of France and the rooms ____________________ (not leave) in a great mess the theft ____________________ (not notice) until last night.

A representative of the insurance company said, "The problem is that the house ____________________ (not secure) an alarm system. However, if the pictures ____________________ (offer) for sale, a reward ____________________ (pay) __________ our company."

Tipp

**Das deutsche *werden* in der nicht passivischen Bedeutung**

Nicht immer hat das Deutsche *werden* passivische Bedeutung, so z. B. bei *alt werden*. Hier muss es dann durch Verben wie *become*, *get* oder *grow (old)* übersetzt werden:
→ *He became rich. He won't grow old, because he smokes too much.*

**4** **Eine junge Frau hat einen Einbruch miterlebt. Ein Polizist muss ihre Aussage aufnehmen. Übertrage die Sätze ins Passiv, wo möglich und sinnvoll.**

The young lady heard a sound in the backyard. She told her brother but he laughed at her. She went into their garden and a man in dark clothes passed her. He asked her, "What are you doing here?" She screamed and all of a sudden all the neighbours switched on the lights. The man hit her on the head, but her dog bit him. Then she didn't know what was happening. But her father called the police. Her scream had woken him up. He found her in the garden. Later she answered all the questions.

Info plus

### Die Polizei in Großbritannien

In Großbritannien gibt es durchschnittlich einen Polizisten *(policeman/policewoman/officer)* pro 400 Einwohner. Es gibt 52 regionale Polizeieinheiten, die jeweils von einem *Chief Constable* geleitet werden. In London sind das die *City Force* und die *Metropolitan Police Force* (Sitz: *New Scotland Yard*).
Polizisten in Großbritannien sind, außer mit einem Knüppel *(truncheon)*, normalerweise nicht bewaffnet.
Der Spitzname *(nickname) bobby*, der den freundlichen und hilfsbereiten Streifenpolizisten *(bobby on his beat)* bezeichnet, erinnert an den Britischen Innenminister *(Home Secretary) Sir Robert Peel* (1788 - 1850), der 1828 die *Metropolitan Police Force*, also *Scotland Yard*, gründete (*Bobby* ist die Kurzform von Robert).
In den USA gibt es die städtische Polizei und die Bezirkspolizei *(Municipal Police* und *County Police)*. Das *FBI (Federal Bureau of Investigation)* trägt keine Uniform *(plain-clothes policemen)* und ist für Bundesgesetze verantwortlich. Der städtischen Polizei steht ein *police chief* vor, der *county police* der *sheriff*. Beide werden von den jeweiligen Bewohnern für von Bundesstaat zu Bundesstaat unterschiedliche Amtsperioden, in der Regel vier Jahre, gewählt.

## Training plus

**7** Übersetze: *Ich werde nächsten Monat 75.*

I'll ___________/___________ seventy-five next month. (2 Möglichkeiten).

**8** *Seem, remain* und *belong* können ______________________ Passiv bilden.

**9** In einem Satz im Aktiv wird der ______________________________

betont, in einem passiven ______________________________.

**10** Die *progressive*-Form des Passiv gibt es nur im …

a) ______________ und im b) ______________________.

**11** Das Objekt im Aktivsatz wird zum ________________ des Passivsatzes.

**12** Wann wird der *by-agent* verwendet? ______________________________

______________________________________________________

______________________________________________________

**1** Es ist Sonntag Morgen. Die Eltern von Sarah, Michael und Susan haben Freunde in London besucht und waren im Theater. Die Kinder haben eine Party gefeiert, doch jetzt müssen sie aufräumen. Setze die Sätze ins Passiv, wo möglich. ___/15

a) Sarah is washing the dishes.

______________________________

b) Michael has carried the plates into the kitchen.

______________________________

c) Only two minutes ago, Susan was vacuum-cleaning the dining-room.

______________________________

______________________________

d) Has Susan cleaned the floor under the sofa?

______________________________

e) After Michael had emptied the dustbin, he dropped it.

______________________________

**2** Übersetze ins Englische. Verwende Passivkonstruktionen, wo dies möglich ist. ___/8

a) Während der Party sagte Michael zu Susans Freundin Laura: „Mein Mofa wird regelmäßig überprüft."

______________________________

______________________________

b) Es wurde gestern von Sarah zur Werkstatt *(garage)* gebracht.

______________________________

______________________________

c) Während sie ins Esszimmer zurückgingen, sahen sie, dass ein Fenster geöffnet wurde.

______________________________

______________________________

d) Hat man dir schon unseren Garten gezeigt?

______________________________

**Gesamtpunktzahl** ___/23

# 3 Modale Hilfsverben: *modal auxiliaries*

**Modale Hilfsverben geben der eigentlichen Handlung, die das Verb ausdrückt, eine Färbung. Sie zeigen an, was eine Person oder Sache (nicht) kann, darf, muss oder soll.**

## 3.1 Häufig vorkommende modale Hilfsverben

Regel

***can – must – mustn't – may – needn't*** **und Ersatzformen**

Modale Hilfsverben erfüllen nicht die volle Funktion eines Verbs. Sie müssen immer von einem Verb begleitet werden.

Vergleiche: *Ich kann Englisch.* → *I can speak English.*

**Modale Hilfsverben verändern ihre Form im Präsens nicht.**

| Hilfsverb | Verwendung | Verneinung |
|---|---|---|
| ***can*** | **Fähigkeit,** etwas zu tun:<br>*She **can** dance well.* | ***cannot, can't*** |
| ***can*** | **Erlaubnis** (oft in einer Frage):<br>***Can** I go to the rock concert tonight?* | ***cannot, can't*** |
| ***must*** | **Notwendigkeit**: *I **must** tell her the truth.* | ***doesn't/ don't have to*** |
| ***have to*** | Ersatzform von ***must***: She **has to** post the letter. | ***doesn't/ don't have to*** |
| ***mustn't*** | Achtung: immer **Verbot**: *You **mustn't** talk.* → *Du darfst nicht sprechen!* | – |
| ***needn't*** | **fehlende Notwendigkeit**: *You **needn't** phone me.*<br>→ *Du brauchst mich nicht anrufen.* | – |

In der Kurzantwort wird das Hilfsverb wiederholt:

*"**Must** I, Miss Sophie?" - "Yes, you **must**, James."*

Die modalen Hilfsverben können nicht alle Zeiten bilden. Möchte man **Vergangenes** oder **Zukünftiges** ausdrücken, muss man **Ersatzformen** verwenden.

| ***modal auxilary*** | **Verwendung** | **Ersatzform *(substitute)*** |
|---|---|---|
| *can* | **Fähigkeit:** *können* | ***be able to do s.th.*** |
| *can, may* | **Erlaubnis:** *dürfen* | ***be allowed to do s.th.*** |
| *must* | **Notwendigkeit:** *müssen* | ***have to do s.th.*** |
| *mustn't* | **Verbot:** *nicht dürfen* | ***be not allowed to do s.th.*** |
| *needn't* | **fehlende Notwendigkeit:** *nicht müssen, nicht brauchen* | ***not have to do s.th.*** |

Das **Passiv** bilden *modal auxiliaries* mit Hilfe des **Infinitiv Passiv** des Vollverbs (Bildung: *be + past participle*), also:

*He may **be asked**. They must **be helped**. The windows needn't **be opened**.*

## 1 Bringe die Sätze in die vorgegebene *tense*.

Example: We can go to the cinema. *(present perfect)*

→ *We have been allowed to go to the cinema.*

a) They must look for Mike's bike. *(will-future)*

______________________________

b) They needn't look at the station. *(simple past)*

______________________________

c) Susan can go to the shopping centre. *(will-future)*

______________________________

d) Tom, you mustn't pick your nose! *(present perfect)*

______________________________

e) I can't phone the police. *(past perfect)*

______________________________

f) She must give back the mobile. *(simple past)*

______________________________

g) Susan cannot be quiet. *(past)*

______________________________

Tipp

**Verneinung von *must***

*You **must** do this.* → Du **musst** dies tun.
*You **mustn't** do this.* → Du **darfst** dies **nicht** tun.

## 2 Setze die richtigen Hifsverben ein:

may · can · must · needn't · may not · must not · cannot

Mike and his family want to go to America in the summer holidays, so he is a bit excited.

Mum, ______________ I ask you a question? - Yes, you ____________. – I like porridge!

______________ I have porridge for breakfast in New York? – No, you ______________.

They only have coffee in New York! - ____________________ I have coffee, too, or ______________ I drink tea in the mornings? - No, you ______________ have coffee. You ______________ have milk in the mornings. - ________ I have a cup of tea now? - Yes, you ______________. Maybe your sisters would like something to drink, too. Why don't you ask them? - ______________ you do that, Mum? They always hit me. - You ____________ go to sleep now, Mike!

It's already very late and we _________________ get up very early tomorrow morning. - ____________ I finish my computer game? - No, you ______________. - Why ______________ *(negative)* I stay here a little longer? My sisters are still up. They ______________ go to bed. - You ______________ yell at me, Mike! - But I'm not yelling! I ____________ speak up, because otherwise you ____________ hear me. Susan and Tina are talking so loudly! - You ______________ say nasty things about your sisters! - I ____________ say anything nice about them! - You are nasty, Mike! You ____________ sleep in the attic!

## 3.2 *Sollen* und *lassen*

Regel

**Das deutsche *sollen***

**Modalhilfsverben** geben den Verben bestimmte **Klangfarben an Bedeutung**. Diese können zu Missverständnissen führen. Im Deutschen verwenden wir das Hilfsverb **sollen** auf verschiedene Weise.

- **Frage** nach einem **Wunsch**, einer **Information** oder einer **Anweisung**
- etwas ist nach **Meinung des Sprechers ratsam**, **moralisch verpflichtend** oder drückt eine **Erwartung** aus
- eine **Anweisung** oder eine **Abmachung** wird weitergegeben
- etwas, was man **gehört** hat, eine **Information** oder ein **Gerücht** wird weitergegeben
- eine **Regel oder Übereinkunft** wird ausgedrückt

## 3 Weise den Sätzen Bedeutungsfärbungen zu.

| | |
|---|---|
| a) Er **soll** in Paris sein. | |
| b) Wo **soll** ich mein Rad hinstellen? | |
| c) Wir **sollen** das Zimmer in der Pause verlassen. | |
| d) Sie **sollten** um 7 Uhr an der Rezeption sein. | |
| e) Du **solltest** diese Wörter lernen. | |

Regel

### *Sollen* im Englischen

| Form | Beispiel | Funktion |
|---|---|---|
| ***be said to*** | *He's **said to** be in Paris.* | *pass on information* |
| ***shall I (we)?*** | *Where **shall we** put our bikes?* → *Wohin sollen wir unsere Räder stellen?* | *ask for a person's wishes or information or instruction directly* |
| ***be to*** | *We **are to** leave our classrom during the break.* → *Wir sollen unser Klassenzimmer … verlassen.* | *an arrangement or instruction is passed on* |
| ***be supposed to*** | *We'**re supposed to** be back at six.* → *Wir sollen um 6 zurück sein.* | *rules, agreements or expectations are expressed* |
| ***should, ought to*** | *You **should** do your homework.* → *Du solltest deine Hausaufgaben machen.* | *s.th. is advisable or a moral obligation in the speaker's opinion* |

## 4 Übersetze und finde das richtige *sollen*. Schreibe ins Heft.

a) Soll ich die Türe aufmachen?
b) Wir sollen nicht mit dem Feuerzeug spielen!
c) Der Hausmeister sollte uns den Garten aufschließen.
d) Dieses Seil soll sicher sein?
e) Du solltest eigentlich die Wörter gelernt haben.
f) Deine Mutter hat gesagt, du sollst um neun im Bett sein.

Regel

### Das deutsche *lassen* im Englischen

- **zulassen/erlauben**: *let s.b. do s.th.* oder *allow s.b. to do s.th.*
  *Her mother let her go to the party.* Ihre Mutter ließ sie zu der Party gehen.
  *Sarah's parents didn't* ***allow*** *her to go to the open-air concert.*
  → Sarahs Eltern ließen sie nicht zum Open-Air-Konzert gehen.
- **jemanden zu etwas veranlassen**: *make s.b. do s.th.*
  *Her mother* ***made*** *her promise not to drink any alcohol at the concert.*
  → Ihre Mutter ließ sich von ihr versprechen, keinen Alkohol zu trinken.
- **etwas vorschlagen**: *let's do s.th.*
  ***Let****'s listen to some reggae music.* → Lasst uns ein wenig Reggae hören.
  *Don't* ***let****'s play only hard rock again.* → Lasst uns nicht wieder nur Hard Rock spielen.
- **veranlassen, dass ein anderer etwas tut**: *have s.th. done (by somebody)*
  *Her parents are going to* ***have*** *her pick****ed*** *up by taxi at midnight.*
  → Ihre Eltern wollen sie um Mitternacht von einem Taxi abholen lassen.
- **etwas zurück-, hinter-, belassen**: *leave s.b./s.th.*
  *He* ***left*** *his bike at the front gate.* → Er ließ sein Rad am Eingangstor stehen.
  *He* ***left*** *his key in the door.* → Er ließ seinen Schlüssel im Türschloss.
  *They* ***left*** *it as it was.* → Sie (be)ließen es wie es war.
- **in Ruhe lassen**: *leave*: ***Leave*** *me alone.* → Lass mich allein.
- **sich Zeit lassen**: *take*: ***Take*** *your time.* → Lass dir ruhig Zeit.

**5** Setze die korrekte Form von *lassen* ein.

a) A woman ______________________ her car in a busy street next to a hotel. (hatte stehen lassen)

b) Two policemen arrived and ____________ their car. (verließen)

c) " ____________________________ be too strict. It' s not really blocking the way." (lass uns nicht)

d) "I think we ________________ towed. We can't ________________ get away with it." (müssen es lassen; den Fahrer lassen)

e) "Look! The driver ____________ the key in the ignition!" (ließ)

f) They ______________ to walk back to their car to ____________ the recovery vehicle called. (ließen sich Zeit; lassen)

g) While they were doing this, the woman came back, drove away and __________ them standing with their mouths open. (ließ)

h) " _____________________ tell this to our boss!" (Lass uns nicht)

## 3.3 Wahrscheinlichkeit

Regel

**Wahrscheinlichkeit**

Wahrscheinlichkeit und Möglichkeit sind oft schwer auseinanderzuhalten, da wir dies im Deutschen nur mit den Hilfsverben *sollen, müssen* und *können* und Adverbien wie *wahrscheinlich, sicherlich* oder *vielleicht* einschränken oder erweitern können. Im Englischen wird die Wahrscheinlichkeit, mit der etwas passieren wird, mit den folgenden Modalhilfsverben und Ersatzformen ausgedrückt.

| Hilfsverb | Wahrscheinlichkeit | *probability* | deutsch |
|---|---|---|---|
| ***might*** | eher unwahrscheinl. | *It is improbable.* | könnte (vielleicht) |
| ***may*** | 50:50 | *It is probable.* | kann (vielleicht ) |
| ***should*** | gut möglich | *It is quite likely.* | sollte eigentlich; müsste |
| ***may very well*** | recht hoch | *It is highly probable.* | … höchstwahrscheinlich … |
| ***will*** | sicher | *It's certain.* | wird … |
| ***going to*** | (wohl) sicher | *It's quite certain.* | … wird (wohl) … |

**6** Eine Wettervorhersage *(A weather forecast)*
Setze die richtige Form für die jeweilige Wahrscheinlichkeit ein.

This is Werner Lamp from the second weather detachment of the Rhein-Main Air Base:

There ____________________ be great weather tomorrow!

It ________________ be sunny in the morning, although there ____________

be a few clouds, especially in the south west, but they are nothing to worry about.

Then there ____________ be sunshine all afternoon and the temperature _______

reach a high of well over 77° degrees, that is 25° celsius. The good weather

____________ continue until the weekend, although there ________________

be some thunderstorms on Friday and Sunday evening.

Info plus

**Temperatur**

Die Temperatur wird in den USA in **Grad Fahrenheit** angegeben. Die Umrechnungsformeln zwischen Grad Celsius und Grad Fahrenheit sind einfach.

**Celsius → *degrees* Fahrenheit:** Celsiuswert · 1,8 + 32

Beispiel: 20 °C · 1,8 = 36; 36 + 32 = 68 °F.

**Grad Fahrenheit → Celsius:** (Fahrenheitwert – 32) : 1,8

Beispiel: 86 °F – 32 = 54; 54 : 1,8 = 30 °C.

## 3.4 Die wichtigsten modalen Hilfsverben im Überblick

| Modalhilfsverb | Bedeutung | Beispiel |
|---|---|---|
| ***can*** | *ability/possibility* | *I **can** do a somersault.* |
| | *permission* | ***Can** I go home now?* |
| | *request* | ***Can** I have a window seat, please?* |
| ***can't*** | *impossibility* | *He **can't** be home, he's just left.* |
| | *inability* | *I **can't** understand Russian.* |
| ***could*** | *past ability* | *He **could** sing well when he was younger.* |
| | *request (polite)* | ***Could** I have a paper bag, please?* |
| | *suggestion* | *You **could** ask the stewardess.* |
| | *<50% possibility* | *I **could** be sick.* |
| ***couldn't*** | *past impossibility* | *He **couldn't** come, he's abroad.* |
| | *past inability* | *I **couldn't** understand Russian.* |
| ***be going to*** | *100% certainty* | *It's **going** to rain any minute.* |
| | *intention/ plan* | *I'**m going** to have a party for my birthday.* |
| ***have to*** | *necessity* | *You **have to** get a passport to travel.* |
| ***may*** | *request* | ***May** I leave?* |
| | *permission* | *You **may** leave.* |
| | *~50 % probability* | *He **may** come.* |
| ***might*** | *>50 % probability* | *He **might** come.* |
| ***must*** | *necessity* | *You **must** get a visa to travel.* |
| | *>90 % certainty* | *He isn't here, he **must** be sick* |
| ***mustn't*** | *prohibition* | *You **must not** smoke in here.* |
| ***shall*** | *suggestion* | ***Shall** I open the door?* |
| ***should*** | *good advice/idea* | *You **should** stay home tonight.* |
| | *70 % probability* | *They **should** have no problem.* |
| ***ought to*** | *good advice/idea* | *I **ought to** stay home tonight.* |
| | *70 % probability* | *They **ought to** have no problem.* |
| ***used to*** | *habitual action* | *I **used to** walk to work in the past, now I take the tram.* |
| ***will*** | *100 % certainty* | *I **will** be there.* |
| | *willing to volunteer* | *This bag is heavy. I'**ll** help you, Madam.* |
| ***would rather*** | *request* | ***Would** you shut the window? **Would** you mind putting the bag in the rack?* |
| | *preference* | *I **would** rather have coffee.* |

**13** Welche Aufgabe übernehmen modale Hilfsverben grundsätzlich?

______________________________________________

**14** Wie bildet man das Präsens Passiv bei modalen Hilfsverben?

______________________________________________

**15** 

Erkläre das *sollen* in dieser Karikatur.

______________________________________________

______________________________________________

______________________________________________

______________________________________________

______________________________________________

**16** Die Verneinung von *must* lautet ______________________.

**17** Wenn man zulässt, dass jemand etwas tut, verwendet man ______________.
Bilde einen Beispielsatz hierzu.

______________________________________________

______________________________________________

**18** Wenn man jemanden zu etwas veranlasst, verwendet man ______________

______________________. Bilde einen Beispielsatz hierzu.

______________________________________________

**19** Muss man ein *modal auxilliary* im *present perfect* verwenden, muss man eine

entsprechende ______________________ verwenden.

z. B.: may → ______________;

can → ______________

**20** *Etwas zurücklassen* heißt im Englischen ______________________

______________________________________________

___/12 **1** Kreuze an, was am besten zu der geschilderten Situation passt.

a) You want a pocket-money rise and you try – by being very nice – to talk your parents into it.
- ☐ Am I to wash Dad's car?
- ☐ Am I supposed to wash Dad's car?
- ☐ Shall I wash Dad's car?

b) You've found an old suitcase in the attic. Fortunately, there was a ring of keys, too.
- ☐ Is this key to open the suitcase?
- ☐ Is this key supposed to open the suitcase?
- ☐ Is this key meant to open the suitcase?

c) Your brother has failed his driving test. Everybody is upset about this catastrophe.
- ☐ He was to study harder.
- ☐ He was supposed to study harder.
- ☐ He should have studied harder.

d) The sun is shining and you are lying next to the pool. You have a Maths test tomorrow.
- ☐ I might go to my room and learn for the Maths test.
- ☐ I should go to my room and learn for the Maths test.
- ☐ I would go to my room and learn for the Maths test.

Jede richtige Lösung, also auch wenn nicht angekreuzt werden darf und auch wirklich nicht angekreuzt wurde, erhält einen Punkt.

___/21 **2** Übersetze und verwende das richtige *lassen*.

a) „Papa, Anne lässt mich nicht in Ruhe!"

______________________________________________

______________________________________________

b) „Könnt ihr nicht einmal ernst sein? Ihr dürft nicht immer so viel Krach machen!"

______________________________________________

______________________________________________

c) „Lasst uns darüber in Ruhe *(calmly)* sprechen."

______________________________________________

______________________________________________

d) „Mike lässt mich immer die ganze Hausarbeit machen. Und er sagt er muss für den Test lernen!"

e) „Lass dir mit deiner Arbeit Zeit."

f) „Ich werde veranlassen, dass Mike dir bei der Hausarbeit hilft. Du musst dich nicht beklagen, Anne."

g) Dann ließ er die Zeitung auf dem Tisch.

Ziehe für jeden Fehler eine Bewertungseinheit ab!

**Gesamtpunktzahl ____/33**

# 4 *Gerunds:* Gerund-Konstruktionen

**Das Gerund ist eine Art substantiviertes Verb. Es entspricht der *-ing*-Form des Verbs und kann in Sätzen wie ein Nomen verwendet werden.**

## 4.1 Das Gerund in verschiedenen Funktionen

Regel

**Bildung und Verwendung des Gerund: das Gerund als Subjekt**

Um Verben als Substantive zu verwenden, hängt man an ihre Stammform im Englischen *-ing* an. So kann das Verb als **Gerund**, also auch in den Eigenschaften eines **Subjekts** verwendet werden: → *Play**ing** the piano is my hobby. Smok**ing** in bed is dangerous.* Dieses Gerund kann durch eine adverbiale Bestimmung (hier: *in bed*) oder ein **Objekt** (hier: *the piano*) erweitert werden.
Ein Gerund kann, wie ein Verb, in **verschiedenen Tenses** (*having played* = gespielt zu haben) und im **Passiv** (*being hated* = gehasst werden; *having been asked* = gefragt worden zu sein) erscheinen und von einem Adverb näher bestimmt werden (*working hard* = hart zu arbeiten, das harte Arbeiten).

**1** Bilde die Gerundformen im Präsens aktiv zu diesen Verben.

| Verb | Gerund Präsens aktiv |
|---|---|
| go | |
| speak | |
| cry | |
| learn | |
| get | |
| play | |
| say | |
| hurry | |
| ride | |

| Verb | Gerund Präsens aktiv |
|---|---|
| write | |
| read | |
| come | |
| think | |
| vote | |
| walk | |
| swim | |
| try | |
| lie | |

Tipp

**Unterscheide Gerund-Formen von Formen des *present progressive*!**

***Sitting*** *in a cafe is fun.* = Gerund
*Tom **is sitting** in a cafe.* Form von ***be*** + ***ing-form*** = ***present progressive***

**2** Übersetze.

a) Skifahren kann gefährlich sein. ______________________

b) Singen macht Spass. ______________________

c) Lesen kann sehr interessant sein. ______________________

d) Lernen ist manchmal langweilig. ______________________

e) Am Strand zu liegen ist mein Lieblingshobby! ______________________

______________________

Regel

**Verwendung des Gerund: Gerund als Objekt**

Das Gerund kann als substantiviertes Verb natürlich auch als **Objekt** verwendet werden: *I like skiing in the Alps. She practises playing the clarinet.*

a) Nach **Verben des Wollens/Mögens/Nicht-Wollens** kann das Gerund in der Funktion eines Objektes stehen: *She **loves** playing the guitar. I **like** swimming in the sea in the evening. He **enjoyed** staying in London for one more week. We **dislike** being asked the same questions. I **hate** doing my homework.*

b) Nach den folgenden Verben (und einigen anderen) muss ein Gerund als Objekt stehen: *admit* (zugeben), *avoid* (vermeiden), *can't help* (nicht anders können), *can't stand/bear* (nicht ausstehen/aushalten können), *deny* (abstreiten), *dislike* (nicht mögen), *finish* (beenden), *go* (z.B. in *go swimming* = schwimmen gehen), *imagine* (sich etw. vorstellen), *keep* (*on*) (weitermachen mit), *mention* (erwähnen), *mind* (stören, etw. dagegen haben), *miss* (verpassen), *practise* (üben), *reject* (zurückweisen), *resist* (widerstehen), *risk* (etwas wagen, riskieren), *suggest* (vorschlagen), *understand* (verstehen), *waste time/money* (Geld/Zeit verschwenden mit).

c) Das Gerund steht **nach allen Adjektiven**, die eine **Präposition** mit sich führen, wie z.B.: *good at, tired of, pround of, angry at, glad of, crazy about, famous for, interested in*: → *She's good at solving mathematical problems. He's famous for asking silly questions.*

d) Nach **Verben,** die eine **Präposition** mit sich führen, steht immer das Gerund: *believe in* (an etwas glauben), *depend on* (abhängen von), *think of* (an etwas denken) und vielen anderen: *He thinks of planning a new expedition.* → Er denkt daran, eine neue Expedition zu planen.

Als **allgemeine Faustregel** gilt: Auf eine Präposition kann fast immer ein Verb in der -***ing***-Form folgen!

**3** Übersetze die Sätze und verwende die Elemente aus der folgenden Liste.

famous for • interested in • think about • proud of • crazy about • enjoy • like • angry about

a) Er liebte es, seine Schwester zu ärgern *(tease)*.

______________________________

b) Sie war manchmal böse darüber, geärgert zu werden, und dachte darüber nach, sich zu rächen *(take revenge)*.

______________________________

______________________________

c) Alle Menschen sind daran interessiert, Neuigkeiten zu erfahren.

______________________________

d) Die Waliser sind berühmt dafür, viel zu singen.

______________________________

e) Sie sind stolz darauf, eine lange Tradition zu haben.

______________________________

Tipp

Im Deutschen wird ein Gerund oft mit *zu* + Infinitiv des Verbs übersetzt:
Er liebt es, die Nacht im Freien **zu verbringen.** → *He loves spending the night outdoors.*

**4** Setze die richtigen Verben ein und verwende *gerunds*.

like • enjoy • be crazy about • be proud of • be good at • to look at
dislike • hate • be not interested in • be not interested in

Harry ______________ field hockey. He is a goalkeeper.

He ______________ balls. He ______________

in the schoolteam. He ______________ it better than

______________ in the classroom. His sister ______________

______________ at horses. She ______________ the

biggest collection of books about horses at the school and she ________________ ________________ any sports.

She ________________________ out and ________________ only ________________ in ________________ her room, except when she can go to Linley's farm to watch the horses.

Their mother would ________________________ a son who is good at school and a daughter who ________________________________ TV.

Regel

**Verwendung des Gerund in Adverbialsätzen**

Folgen Gerunds einer **Präposition als adverbiale Bestimmung**, so stehen sie meist für einen adverbialen Nebensatz oder einen mit *und* verbundenen Hauptsatz. Sowohl der verkürzte Hauptsatz, wie auch der verkürzte Nebensatz haben dann das gleiche Subjekt wie der Hauptsatz:

***After he had left** school he worked at a restaurant.* → ***After leaving** school he worked at a restaurant.*

***He** crossed **the street** and didn't look.* → ***He** crossed the street **without** looking.*

**Präpositionen, nach denen das Gerund steht:**

*after* (nach), *apart from* (außer), *because of* (wegen), *before* (ehe, bevor, vor), *by* (dadurch dass; indem), *for* (dafür, für, dass; weil), *in* (indem), *in spite of* (trotz, obwohl), *instead of* (anstatt), *on* (als, gleich nachdem), *without* (ohne zu).

Tipp

Nach *after* verwendet man eher selten die Vergangenheitsform des Gerund (*having left*): Besser: *After leaving school* … als: *After having left* …

Der verkürzte Nebensatz (Gerund) und der Hauptsatz werden nicht durch ein Komma getrennt.

**5** Verkürze die unterstrichenen Teile mithilfe einer Präposition + Gerund.

a) After he had washed his face he brushed his teeth.

________________________________________________

b) Because he was always late he never had breakfast.

________________________________________________

c) <u>Although he was hungry</u> he had to go to his boss first.

______________________________________________

d) <u>He left his office and</u> went directly to the cafeteria.

______________________________________________

e) He went to the counter <u>and didn't look around.</u>

______________________________________________

**6** Übersetze und bilde Gerund-Konstruktionen.

a) Sein Chef stand hinter ihm und sagte …

______________________________________________

b) Außer dass Sie jeden Tag zu spät kommen, verbringen sie jeden Morgen eine halbe Stunde in der Cafeteria!

______________________________________________

c) Kommen Sie noch einmal in mein Büro, bevor Sie das Haus verlassen.

______________________________________________

d) Anstatt hier zu essen sollten Sie arbeiten.

______________________________________________

e) Gehen Sie in ihr Büro, ohne einen Umweg *(detour)* zu machen.

______________________________________________

Regel

**Verwendung des Gerund: Gerund mit eigenem Sinn-Subjekt**

Manchmal tauchen im Gerundteil eigene (Sinn-)Subjekte (fett gedruckte Teile) auf. *Sarah didn't like* ***Mike*** *leaving for a year.* → Sarah wollte nicht, dass Mike für ein Jahr weggeht. *She didn't mind* ***him*** *leaving for a week.* → Es machte ihr nichts aus, dass er für eine Woche weggeht. *She insisted on* ***his*** *coming back after one month.* → Sie bestand darauf, dass er nach einem Monat zurückkam.
*She was tired of* ***Mike's*** *working abroad.* → Sie hatte es satt, dass Mike im Ausland arbeitete.

Das **Sinn-Subjekt des englischen Gerundsatzes** kann sowohl eine **Person im Objekt- oder im Possessiv-Fall** sein (bei Dingen nur Objekt-Fall), als auch ein **Pronomen im Objekt-Fall** (***him***, ***me*** etc.) oder ein **Possessivbegleiter** (***his***, ***your*** etc.). In der Umgangssprache wird die Objektform bevorzugt. In formellen Texten verwendet man eher den Genitiv bzw. den Possessivbegleiter.

Im Deutschen wird diese Konstruktion gewöhnlich durch einen ***dass*-Satz** wiedergegeben.

Tipp

**used to**

*I <u>used</u> to be a rockstar in 1980.* → pflegte zu sein; war früher einmal
*He <u>is used</u> to drinking lots of tea.* → es gewohnt sein, etwas zu tun
*This sponge <u>is used</u> to clean/for cleaning the floors.* → zu etwas verwendet werden

**7** Mrs Jones is having a bad day. Vervollständige die Sätze und verwende Gerundkonstruktionen mit eigenem Sinn-Subjekt.

a) Mrs Jones is interested in ______________________________.

b) She insists on ______________________________.

c) She doesn't like her ______________________________.

d) She can't cope with ______________________________.

e) She complains about ______________________________.

f) Mr Jones is used to ______________________________.

Info plus

**Down Under**

Ein *Great South Land* war schon lange Zeit vorher vermutet worden, jedoch erst im 17. Jahrhundert entdeckten Seeleute aus den Niederlanden die riesige Insel, die wir heute Australien nennen. 1770 erforschte Captain Cook die Ostküste, die er New South Wales nannte und beanspruchte den neuen Kontinent als britische Kolonie. Die ersten Siedler, die sich 1787 auf die 12 000 Seemeilen lange Reise machten, taten dies nicht freiwillig. Es waren Sträflinge, die zu **transportation for life**, also lebenslanger Verbannung verurteilt waren. Im 18. Jahrhundert hatte England die härtesten Gesetze Europas, daher waren die Gefängnisse überfüllt. Der Transport von Gefangenen nach Australien endete erst 1840.

## 4.2 Gerund oder Infinitiv?

Regel

**Gerund oder to-Infinitiv?**

Manche Verben, wie z.B. *love* or *like* können ein Gerund *oder* einen Infinitiv anschließen. In vielen Fällen ist der Bedeutungsunterschied nur gering, bei einigen Verben ist jedoch Vorsicht geboten:

- *She'll never* ***forget*** *visit**ing** Paris.* (… besucht zu haben) → Handlung vorbei!
  *She* ***forgot to talk*** *to him.* (… zu sprechen) → Handlung gleichzeitig!
- *I* ***remember*** *read**ing** it.* (… gelesen zu haben) → Handlung abgeschlossen!
  *I must* ***remember to learn*** *for the test.* (… zu lernen) → Bezug zur Zukunft!
- *He* ***regretted*** *leav**ing** her.* (… verlassen zu haben) → Bezug Vergangenheit!
  *He* ***regretted to have to leave*** *her* (… sie zu verlassen) → Bezug Gegenwart!
- *He* ***went on*** *talk**ing** too fast.* (… sprach weiterhin zu schnell) → mit der gleichen/selben Handlung weitermachen!
- *After K2 he* ***went on to climb*** *Mount Everest.* (… machte er weiter mit) → mit einer neuen Handlung beginnen!
- *I finally* ***stopped*** *smok**ing*** (… mit dem Rauchen aufgehört) → etwas beenden!
  *He* ***stopped to look*** *around.* (… um sich umzusehen) → eine Handlung beenden, um eine andere zu beginnen!
- *The car broke down and that* ***meant*** *walk**ing**.* (… bedeutete, dass wir laufen mussten.) → eine Handlung hat die Folge, dass etwas getan werden muss!
- *He* ***meant to repair*** *the car before we left.* (Er wollte eigentlich das Auto reparieren …) → etwas zu tun beabsichtigen!
  *I* ***tried playing*** *the trombone once but as much as I* ***tried to produce*** *a sound I didn't succeed.* → *try doing* = ausprobieren; *try to do* = sich bemühen etwas zu tun.

Gruppe *hate, like, love, prefer*

- *I hate being laughed at. He loves getting up early.* → allgemeine Feststellung!
- *She hated to be laughed at when she was giving the speech. We'd love to see you again tonight.* → besondere Situation, Einzelfall!

## 8 Infinitiv oder Gerund? Setze die richtige Form ein.

Susan had a terrible toothache. Although she had taken a pill, her bad tooth went on _____________ (hurt). She tried _____________ (phone) her dentist _____________ (make) an appointment but found out that he was on holiday.

"Try _______________ (talk) to Dr Alb." Her colleague advised her. - "I don't want _____________________(leave) my old dentist, but I would really love _____________ (get rid) of my tooth-ache. As usual, her tooth stopped ___________________ (ache) after she had made the appointment. She had so much work that she forgot _____________ (go). When in the evening her toothache started again Susan regretted _____________________ (forget) her appointment. The next morning, on her way to work she stopped ________________ (call) at Dr Alb's, "I meant ___________________ (be) here in time yesterday but my tooth had stopped ___________________ (hurt). I hate _____________ (disappoint) people."

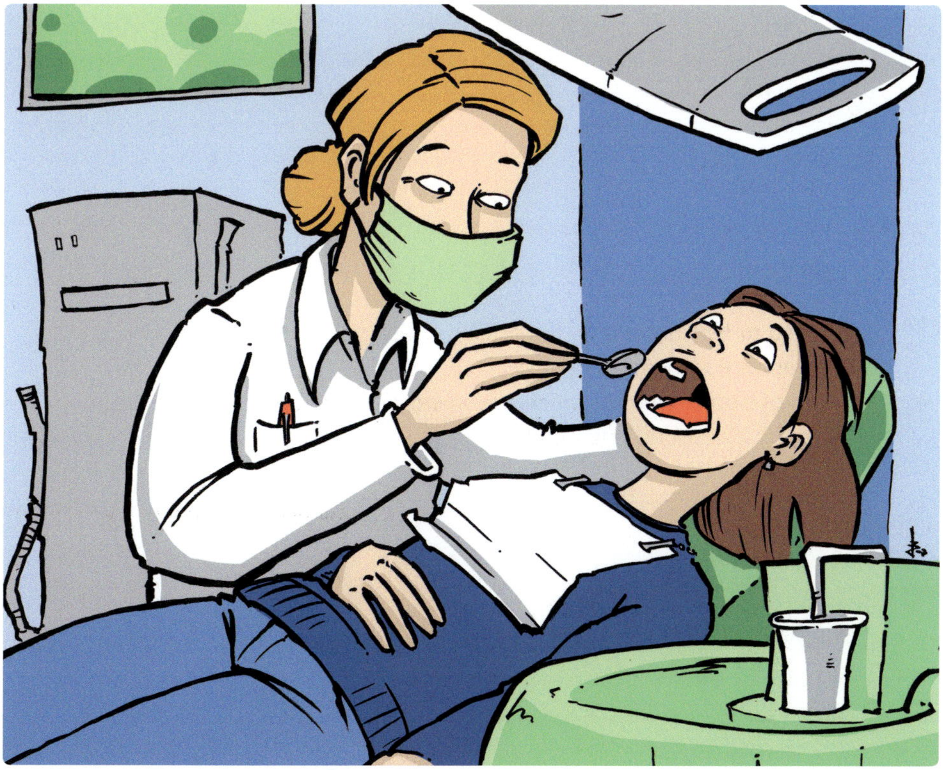

**21** *Gerunds* können wie Substantive in einem Satz die Funktion eines

______________ oder eines ______________ übernehmen.

**22** Übersetze.

a) They were used to working hard. ______________________________

______________________________

b) Water is used to extinguish fire. ______________________________

______________________________

c) They used to be pilots. ______________________________

______________________________

**23** Bilde das Gerund im Präsens Passiv für die folgenden Verben.

a) beat: ______________________________

b) unload: ______________________________

c) respect: ______________________________

**24** Ergänze die richtige Präposition.

a) good ______________

b) tired ______________

c) depend ______________

d) interested ______________

**25** a) They stopped to smoke.
b) They stopped smoking.

Welche Handlung ist die gesündere? Erkläre warum. ______________________________

______________________________

______________________________

**26** Stehen *hate, love, like, prefer* mit einem to-Infinitiv, beschreiben sie einen

______________.

**1** Setze die richtige Form ein und ergänze Präpositionen und Sinn-Subjekte wo notwendig. ___/30

a) I didn't feel like ____________, so I suggested ____________ the bus. (walk; take)

b) I remember ____________ to him. (talk)

c) I'm tired of ____________ of crooks who are rewarded instead of ____________ punished. (hear; be)

d) Would you mind ____________ again? I forgot ____________ my hearing-aid. (she, answer; switch on)

e) If something is worth ____________, it is worth ____________ it well. (do; do)

f) There's nothing like ____________ music as a means of ____________. (make; relax)

g) I hope you don't mind ____________ you so late, but I don't want to go on holiday without ____________ you on your promotion. (I, ring; congratulate)

h) Try ____________ that, it isn't worth ____________ about. (forget; worry)

i) The boys used ____________ swimming, but now they only enjoy ____________ in front of their computers. (enjoy; sit)

j) In spite of ____________ to him for two hours, I didn't succeed in ____________ him. I said, "Keep ____________ things like that and you won't ever find a decent job. But it's no use ____________ you. You will never start ____________ to me. You are simply not interested in ____________ your situation!" (talk; convince; say; tell; listen; improve)

k) "She regretted ____________ her ill daughter at home alone, but she had to go ____________". (have to leave; shop)

l) He was accused ____________ the necklace but denied ____________ it. (steal; take)

m) After ____________ through the countryside for two hours, Mr Miller stopped ____________ the children ____________ for a while. (drive; let; play)

**Gesamtpunktzahl** ___/30

# 5 *Participles:* Partizipialkonstruktionen

Partizipien *(participles)* gehören wie Gerund- und Infinitiv-Konstruktionen zu den infiniten Verbformen, d.h. man muss ihre Formen nicht an Person *(person)*, Ein- oder Mehrzahl *(numerus)* oder die Zeitform *(tense)* anpassen.

## 5.1 Partizipien in verschiedenen Funktionen

Regel

**Die Bildung der Partizipien**

Das **Partizip** wird auch **Verbaladjektiv** genannt. Es existiert als ***present participle*** und als ***past participle*** im Aktiv und im Passiv.

Das ***present participle*** bildet man mit der *-ing*-Form des Verbs (Stammform des Verbs + *-ing*), das ***past participle*** bei regelmäßigen Verben mit *-ed (having* + Stammform des Verbs + *-ed*). Bei unregelmäßigen Verben: *having* + dritte zu lernende Verbform (z.B. *sing* - *sang* - ***sung***).

Achte auf die Unterschiede zwischen Aktiv und Passiv!

| | **present participle** | **past participle** |
|---|---|---|
| **active voice** | asking | having asked |
| **passive voice** | (being) asked | (having been) asked |

**1** Bilde Partizipien.

| **infinitive** | **present participle** | **past participle** |
|---|---|---|
| sell (Aktiv) | | |
| write (Passiv) | | |
| cheat (Aktiv) | | |
| switch on (Passiv) | | |
| drive (Aktiv) | | |
| help (Passiv) | | |
| waste (Aktiv) | | |
| print (Passiv) | | |
| buy (Aktiv) | | |

Regel

**_Present participles_ als Adjektive/Adverbien und nach bestimmten Verbgruppen**

- ***Present participles*** können **als Adjektive und Adverbien** verwendet und damit auch **gesteigert** werden: *They complained about* ***rising*** *prices. They enjoyed* ***most surprising*** *comfort.*
- ***Present participles*** folgen **Verben der Sinneswahrnehmung** (*verbs of perception*), z.B. *see, hear, watch, notice*: *I* ***saw*** *the hooligans* ***running*** *down the street.* Ich sah, wie die Hooligans die Straße hinunter liefen.
  Im Deutschen steht hier oft ein Adverbialsatz, bei dem das **direkte Objekt des englischen Satzes** zum **Subjekt des deutschen Nebensatzes** wird.
  *He saw* ***her*** *opening the door.* Er sah, wie **sie** die Tür öffnete.
  Manchmal kann aber auch die deutsche Satzstruktur der englischen sehr ähneln: *I saw* ***her*** *standing there.* Ich sah **sie** da stehen.
- Nach **Verben der Bewegung und Ruhe** (*verbs of movement and rest*), z.B. *sit, stand, lie, remain, stay, come, go, walk, run, arrive, return*, steht das *present participle* als prädikative Ergänzung zum Subject. Diese Konstruktion wird im Deutschen meist als Nebensatz mit *wobei* bzw. *indem* oder als Hauptsatz realisiert. *The hooligans came* ***rushing*** *down the street. They stood there* ***watching*** *the sea.* Die Hooligans kamen die Straße herabgeeilt. Sie standen da und beobachteten das Meer.

**2** Übersetze und verwende *present participles*.

a) Fallende Preise sind schlecht für das Geschäft.

________________________________________

b) Catweazle blieb ruhig sitzen. Touchwood hörte ihn atmen. Die Normannen kamen durch den Wald gerannt und suchten den alten Zauberer. Sie beobachteten, wie er aus dem Fenster kletterte. Dann sahen sie, wie er ins Wasser sprang.

________________________________________

________________________________________

________________________________________

________________________________________

c) Es war ein bewegender Anblick. Sie standen vor dem Bahnhof und schauten einander an. Dann verharrten (*stay*) sie und hielten sich ganz fest. Sie bemerkte jedoch nicht, wie er nervös auf seine Uhr schaute. Er hatte gehört, wie der Zug abfuhr.

________________________________________

Regel

***Present participles*** **– weitere Funktionen**

- ***Present participles*** **verkürzen Relativsätze im Aktiv:** *The man* ***standing*** *over there is a spy.* Der Mann, der dort drüben steht, ist ein Spion.
- ***Present participles*** **verkürzen Adverbialsätze:** ***Sleeping*** *too long he missed his bus.* Da er zu lange geschlafen hatte, verpasste er den Bus.
  Normalerweise ersetzen Partizipien adverbiale Nebensätze der **Zeit** oder des **Grundes**. Ob es sich um einen adverbialen Nebensatz der Zeit oder des Grundes handelt, ergibt sich meist deutlich aus dem Kontext. Soll ein andersartiger Nebensatz durch ein *present participle* ersetzt werden, wird dies mit einer Konjunktion verdeutlicht: *After* ***leaving*** *the house, he heard the noise.* Nachdem er das Haus verlassen hatte, hörte er das Geräusch.
  ***Though not having*** *much time, he helped her.* Obwohl er wenig Zeit hatte, half er ihr.
- ***Present participles*** können einen **zweiten Hauptsatz überflüssig** machen. Dieser wird im Deutschen mit *und* angeschlossen: *They sat there* ***laughing****.* Sie saßen da und (sie) lachten.
- ***Present participles*** können ein eigenes Sinn-Subjekt verkörpern: ***The weather being*** *bad they couldn't go out.* Weil das Wetter schlecht war, konnten sie nicht ausgehen. Die Partizipialkonstruktion mit eigenem Sinn-Subjekt steht für einen Nebensatz oder zwei Hauptsätze. Diese Konstruktion findet man allerdings nur in der gehobenen Schriftsprache.
  ***– with + noun + V-ing:*** Auch hier hat das Partizip ein eigenes Sinn-Subjekt. Diese Konstruktion findet man auf allen Stilebenen. Das englische *with* wird praktisch **nie** ins Deutsche **übersetzt**: ***With*** *the weather* ***being*** *bad they didn't leave the hotel.* Weil das Wetter schlecht war, verließen sie das Hotel nicht.

**3** Verkürze die Sätze mithilfe von *present participles.*

a) After the alarm-clock had rung Mr Strange left the bedroom very quietly, as he didn't want to wake up his wife.

b) Neo reached the end of the building and turned around sharply. He jumped towards Agent Smith and tried to hit him.

______________________________

______________________________

c) As he didn't want to leave Morpheus in the hands of Zion, he surrendered to Agent Smith.

______________________________

______________________________

d) Although Agent Smith kills Neo, he does not succeed.

______________________________

e) After Trinity had kissed Neo, he regained his powers.

______________________________

______________________________

f) The machines took over the power and people became slaves.

______________________________

**4** Verbinde die Sätze mit einer Partizipialkonstruktion.

a) Tom moved to LA. He hoped to find a better job there.

______________________________

b) John hit the curb. Then he fell off his bike.

______________________________

c) Al wanted to go home. He closed the shoe shop early.

______________________________

Regel

***Past participles***

- **verkürzen Relativsätze im Passiv:** *Cars* ***made*** *in Japan are quite reliable.* Autos, **die** in Japan **hergestellt werden**, sind ziemlich zuverlässig.
- **verkürzen Adverbialsätze:** ***Hated*** *by most pupils the teacher had a quiet life.* Weil er von den meisten Schülern gehasst wurde, hatte der Lehrer ein ruhiges Leben.
- folgen Konstruktionen mit *have* im Sinn von **jemanden etwas tun lassen**: *I had my hair* ***cut****.* Ich **ließ** mir die Haare schneiden.
- folgen **Verben der Sinneswahrnehmung (verbs of perception)**, z. B. *see, hear* und *feel: I* ***felt*** *my arm* ***touched****.* Ich fühlte, wie mein Arm berührt wurde.

**5** Verkürze die unterstrichenen Teile mit einem *past participle*.

a) He was left alone in the dark, so he started to cry.

c) Because he was born on the fourth of July, he was called Americano.

c) After he had been knocked out twice, my friend stopped boxing.

Info plus

**Die Römer in Britannien**

Die Römer hatten lange Handelsbeziehungen mit Britannien, bevor sie es im Jahr 43 vor Christus eroberten. Bis zum Jahr 410 nach Christus, als die Römer die britischen Inseln verließen, war Britannien eine der reichsten und wertvollsten Provinzen des römischen Reichs. Die keltische Bevölkerung hatte die römische Lebensart angenommen und sich im Laufe der Jahrhunderte mit ihren Besatzern vermischt.
Aufgrund ihres Reichtums war die ehemalige Provinz Britannia auch für andere Völker interessant, sodass z.B. Wikinger, Angeln und Sachsen einwanderten und durch ihren Einfluss einen Großteil der kelto-romanischen Kultur überprägten.
Heute gibt es nur noch wenige römische Bauwerke in Großbritannien, unter ihnen *Hadrian's Wall*, einen Leuchtturm bei Dover und die römischen Bäder in *Bath*.
In der Sprache erkennt man heute noch viele Wörter römischen Ursprungs, darunter in Städtenamen die Endungen *-cester*, *-chester* und *-caster* vom lateinischen *castra*, was *befestigtes Lager* bedeutet und auch im Deutschen im Wort *Kastell* weiterlebt.

**27** Das *Present participle* findet man nach folgenden Verbarten:

*verbs* ______________________________

und *verbs* ______________________________

**28** Nenne jeweils drei Beispiele für die beiden in 27 genannten Verbgruppen.

a) ______________________________

b) ______________________________

**29** *Surprisingly* ist ein ____________, das aus einem *participle* gebildet wurde.

**30** Ersetzt ein *participle* einen Adverbialsatz und es folgt keiner Konjunktion, so ergibt sich aus dem Kontext, ob es einen Nebensatz der

____________ oder des ____________ ersetzt.

**31** Übersetze: *He rode into the night with the moon shining brightly.*

______________________________

**32** *Past participles* können Relativsätze im ____________ verkürzen.

**33** *jemanden etwas tun lassen* wird im Englischen mit folgender Konstruktion

ausgedrückt: ______________________________

______________________________

___/18 **1** Übersetze und verwende, wo möglich, Partizipialkonstruktionen.

a) Gestern abend wollte ich meinen Freund Stefan besuchen.

b) Als wir im Wagen saßen, fragte ich meine Frau, ob sie die Gartentür abgeschlossen hatte.

c) Da meine Frau es vergessen hatte, ging sie schnell zurück.

d) Nachdem ich zehn Minuten gewartet hatte, wurde ich ungeduldig und ging ebenfalls ins Haus zurück.

e) Als ich an der Türe stand, hörte ich, wie mein Name gerufen wurde.

f) Ich sah durch das Fenster und bemerkte zwei Männer, die mit meiner Frau redeten.

g) Ich ergriff *(grab)* einen Spaten *(spade)*, der neben der Türe stand und rannte hinein.

h) Als ich das Wohnzimmer erreicht hatte, sah ich die Männer durch den Garten verschwinden.

i) Die Männer waren Polizisten, die von Haus zu Haus gingen, um die Leute vor einem Einbrecher zu warnen.

2 Verkürze bzw. verbinde die Sätze mit Partizipialkonstruktionen. ___/22

a) Since I am quite forgetful, I have to write a lot of little notes.

______________________________

b) The small yellow pieces of paper, which hang everywhere in our house, can also be more of a curse than a help.

______________________________

______________________________

c) After I had found one, which was sticking in the pocket of my winter coat two weeks ago, I asked my wife: "Did you write a post-it which says 'STOP!'?"

______________________________

______________________________

d) My wife looked at the yellow piece of paper and said, "This is not my handwriting!"

______________________________

e) The post-it was laid down on the piano. It was looked at at least 10 times per day. It became an ominous threat.

______________________________

f) We wondered about it every day and just couldn't remember what had to stop.

______________________________

g) Yesterday I drove to the airport and  picked up my brother, who had come back from a four-week trip to Hawaii.

______________________________

h) He was deeply tanned and was wearing a colourful shirt, and he felt very cold.

______________________________

i) As he was very tired and jetlagged he went to bed at once.

______________________________

j) When I woke up the next morning I saw my brother. He was standing next to the piano and laughing.

______________________________

k) He had borrowed my overcoat before his flight and left the reminder in its pocket.

______________________________

Gesamtpunktzahl ___/40

# 6 *Infinitives:* Konstruktionen mit Infinitiven

**Wie das Gerund und die Partizipien, so gehören auch die Infinitiv-Konstruktionen im Englischen zu den infiniten Formen. Infinite Formen sind nicht veränderbar, d.h. sie werden nicht an die Person, den Numerus oder das Tempus angepasst.**

## 6.1 Infinitive in verschiedenen Funktionen

Regel

***to-infinitive*** **und** ***bare infinitive***

Im Englischen unterscheidet man zunächst einmal **zwei Infinitivarten**, den Infinitiv **mit** vorangestelltem *to* (***to-infinitive***) und den **ohne** *to* (***bare infinitive***):

*He'd like* ***to see*** *the girl tomorrow.* → *to-infinitive*

*She can* ***leave*** *her luggage in the hotel lobby.* → *bare infinitive*

Außerdem unterscheidet man nach **Aktiv** und **Passiv**, **Präsens** und **Perfekt** die folgenden vier Formen:

| | Aktiv | Passiv |
|---|---|---|
| **Präsens** | *(to) carry* | *(to) be carried* |
| **Perfekt** | *(to) have carried* | *(to) have been carried* |

Der **Infinitiv Präsens** hat auch eine ***progressive form***. Sie wird mit *be + -ing* gebildet:

*Steven must* ***be tidying*** *up his room now.*

**1** Bilde die folgenden Infinitiv-Formen.

***get*** (Präsens, Aktiv, mit *to*) ________________

***paint*** (Perfekt, Passiv, *bare*) ________________

***sing*** (Präsens, Passiv, *bare*) ________________

***buy*** (Perfekt, Aktiv, mit *to*) ________________

***find*** (Präsens, Aktiv, *progressive*, *bare*) ________________

***check*** (Präsens, Passiv, *bare*) ________________

***put*** (Präsens, Aktiv, *progressive*, mit *to*) ________________

***enter*** (Perfekt, Passiv, mit *to*) ________________

Regel

### *to*-Infinitiv nach Adjektiven, Superlativen, Ordnungszahlen und *the only*

- Der ***to***-Infinitiv steht nach Adjektiven und deren Steigerungsformen:
  *It seems difficult **to learn** the rules for rugby. It seems more difficult **to learn** the rules for cricket. It is most problematic **to understand** American football tactics.*
- ***to***-Infinitive stehen auch nach **Superlativen**, **Ordnungszahlen** und ***the only***:
  *It was the most famous band **to perform** at the festival. She was the third **to be attacked** by the huge dog. This was the only chance **to enter** the room without being seen.*

Verwendet man *the only* im Plural, so wird daraus ***the only ones***: *We were the only ones to get access to the castle.*

## 2 Übersetze. Schreibe in dein Heft.

a) Herr Miller war der zweite, der von der Schlange gebissen wurde.
b) Es ist sehr leicht eine Giftschlange von einer Blindschleiche *(slow worm)* zu unterscheiden.
c) Waren sie die einzigen, die am Töpferkurs *(pottery course)* teilnahmen?
d) Sie wird sicherlich ihre Anstellung verlieren. (sicherlich – hier: *be certain*)

Regel

### *to*-Infinitiv nach Fragewörtern und *whether*

Der ***to***-Infinitiv kann nach Fragewörtern wie *where, when, who, why* etc. und nach *whether* stehen. Er ersetzt dann meistens einen komplizierteren Neben- oder Gliedsatz:

*I'm not sure who **to ask**.* → Ich weiß nicht, wen ich **fragen soll**.
*Can you tell me where **to find** him?* → Kannst du mir sagen, **wo** ich ihn **finden kann**?
*She didn't tell me when **to meet** at the bus stop.* → Sie sagte mir nicht, **wann** wir uns an der Haltestelle **treffen sollten**.
*He doesn't know whether **to walk** or go by bike.* → Er weiß nicht, **ob** er **laufen** oder **mit dem Fahrrad fahren soll**.

## 3 Setze die passenden Fragewörter oder *whether* und die Infinitive ein.

Yesterday my sister couldn't decide ________________ ________________ to the cinema or ________________ her friends *(go; meet)*. First, she wanted ________________ the new Harry Potter film, but she didn't know ________________ ________________ into town *(see; get)*. So she decided ________________ her best friend but either of them was able to find out ______________

______________ the film *(phone; watch)*. My mother finally told them

______________________________ *(go)*.

I really didn't know ______________ ______________ them or not *(join)*.

Regel

**to-Infinitiv nach Nomen und *somebody/something***

**Statt eines Relativsatzes mit modalem Hilfsverb** kann im Englischen **nach Nomen** oder ***somebody/something*** der **to-Infinitiv** stehen:

*He's the man **who can rescue** the sailors.* → *He's the man **to rescue** the sailors.*

*The camper van **that must be driven back** to Los Angeles is parked behind the supermarket.* → *The camping car **to be driven back** to Los Angeles is parked behind the supermarket.*

*At the moment I don't know anybody **that I could tell** the secret to.* → *At the moment I don't know anybody **to tell** the secret to.*

*She's somebody **that has to be helped** quickly.* → *She's somebody **to be helped** quickly.*

**4** Wandle die unterstrichenen Teile unter Verwendung von *to-infinitives* um.

a) Charles Lindbergh was one of the most courageous pilots that you can find in the American history of aviation.

______________________________________________

b) He was somebody who could always put his dreams into reality within a short period of time.

______________________________________________

c) Although Lindbergh had not had much experience, he thought of himself as the man that might be able to fly a solo across the Atlantic Ocean for the first time in history.

______________________________________________

Info plus

### Charles Lindbergh

Charles Lindbergh gelang im Mai 1927 die erste Nonstop-Überquerung des Atlantiks von New York nach Paris im Alleinflug in seinem berühmten Flugzeug *Spirit of St. Louis*. Zuvor hatten die beiden amerikanischen Piloten Alcock und Brown den Atlantik bereits bezwungen - aber eben zu zweit. Um möglichst viel Gewicht und damit auch Treibstoff zu sparen, hatte Lindbergh auf ein Funkgerät und Navigationsinstrumente verzichtet und seinen Flug damit zu einem der gefährlichsten Abenteuer der Luftfahrgeschichte werden lassen.

Regel

### *to*-Infinitiv nach *for* + Nomen/Pronomen

Häufig steht im Englischen die Konstruktion ***for*** **+ Nomen/Pronomen +** ***to*****-Infinitiv**: Die Infinitiv-Konstruktion erleichtert auch hier grundsätzlich den Satzbau, indem sie zwei Hauptsätze in einem vereint:
*This is your birthday present. You can unwrap it during the flight to New York.* → *This is your birthday present* ***to be unwrapped*** *during the flight to New York.*

*The bus was very slow for them. They missed the plane.* → *The bus was too slow for them to get on the plane in time.*

*Thousands of fans are waiting for the soccer star. He will arrive.* → *Thousands of fans are waiting for the soccer star to arrive.*

Regel

### *to*-Infinitiv nach Verben des (Nicht-)Wünschens und (Nicht-)Wollens, des Zulassens und Veranlassens und Denkens, Sagens und Vermutens

- Nach **Verben des Wünschens/Wollens/Nichtwünschens** und **Nichtwollens** kann folgende Konstruktion stehen: **Verb +** ***want/would like***/etc. **+ Objekt +** ***to*****-Infinitiv**:
  *My sister* ***wants (hates) my brother to do*** *her homework.* Meine Schwester ***will*** **(hasst es), dass mein Bruder** ihre Hausaufgaben **macht**.

  In solchen Sätzen wird klar, dass das Subjekt des Satzes (*My sister*) sich vom Objekt des Satzes (*her brother*) etwas wünscht (nicht wünscht).
- Nach **Verben des Zulassens und Veranlassens**, z. B. *allow, permit, cause, tell, order, expect*, folgt im Englischen oft ein **Objekt** und ein ***to*****-Infinitiv**:
  *His uncle* ***allowed him to watch*** *the late-night movie, but he also* ***expected him to go*** *to bed straight after it. Sein Onkel erlaubte ihm, den Spätfilm anzusehen, aber er erwartete von ihm auch, dass er danach sofort ins Bett gehen würde.*
- Nach Verben des **Denkens, Sagens und Vermutens**, z. B. *suppose, imagine, believe, considers, know*, folgt im Englischen oft ein **Objekt** und ein ***to*****-Infinitiv**:
  *She* ***considered him to be*** *rich.* → *Sie* ***dachte***, ***er sei*** *reich.*

**5** Übersetze. Schreibe in dein Heft.

Für einen jungen Menschen ist es schwierig, die Vorteile eines ordentlich aufgeräumten Zimmers zu verstehen. Auch für mich war es nie leicht, dies einzusehen, aber für meinen Sohn ist es schrecklich genug, in einem aufgeräumten Zimmer zu sitzen. Ständig wartet er darauf, dass jemand den Boden staubsaugt.

Tipp

***want to do s.th. – want s.b. to do s.th.***

Aufgepasst, die folgenden Strukturen sind ähnlich, unterscheiden sich aber in ihrer Bedeutung beträchtlich:
*Robert wanted to marry her.* → Robert wollte sie heiraten.
*Robert wanted her to marry.* → Robert wollte, dass sie heiratete.

**6** Übersetze in deinem Heft.

a) Peter möchte, dass sein Bruder ihm den Brief laut vorliest.

b) Er möchte aber nicht, dass der Brief von seinen Eltern gelesen wird.

c) Deshalb erwartet er von seinem Bruder, dass dieser den Brief unter seinem Bett versteckt.

## 6.2 Infinitive ohne *to*

Regel

***bare infinitives***

Infinitive **ohne vorangestelltes *to*** kommen in folgenden Fällen vor:

- in den Bedeutungen von **lassen/veranlassen/jdn. dazu bringen, dass …** (siehe Kapitel 3): *The policeman made the driver **walk** along a yellow line. Please, let me **carry** your suitcase. Have him **solve** the problem. Let him **go**!*
- nach **den modalen Hilfsverben** mit **Ausnahme** von ***ought***: *He can **walk** along the line. She must **carry** her suitcase.* Aber: *He ought **to carry** her bag.*
- nach ***had better***, ***why not*** und ***would rather***: *She**'d better talk** to me. Sie hätte besser mit mir gesprochen. **Why not go** for a walk? Warum gehen wir nicht spazieren? She **would** ('d) **rather listen to the song**. Sie würde lieber das Lied hören.*

## 7 Füge ein *to* ein wo dies notwendig ist.

Birch Aquarium is a wonderful place ______ discover on your holiday. There is so much ______ see about the great variety of Pacific marine life. There are more than 60 habitats ______ explore. We let you ______ enter the world of sharks, seahorses and living coral reefs. It's just great ______ dive into oceanographic exhibitions. We present the mysteries of the ocean ______ be seen in our multimedia shows. It is quite easy ______ touch tidepool creatures in living tidepools. Birch Aquarium is the best public exploration center ______ visit in the west. For more than a century our sealife museum has delighted San Diego's residents and visitors ______ come into contact with the wonders of the ocean. Let's ______ enjoy delicious sandwich and salad creations, beverages and snacks at the Splash Café. It will be a delightful experience ______ choose from a unique selection of marine-themed clothing in the gift shop. There you can also ______ get souvenirs and books. Let us ______ convince you of about this magnificent world!

Tipp

### Aufgepasst bei Verben der Sinneswahrnehmung!

Bei den Verben der Sinneswahrnehmung gibt es zwei ähnliche Konstruktionen, die jedoch unterschiedliche Bedeutung haben.

| Verb + Objekt + *bare infinitive* | Verb + Objekt + V-ing |
|---|---|
| *I saw him **cross** the street.*<br>→ *Ich sah, **dass** er die Straße überquerte.* | *I saw him **crossing** the street.*<br>→ *Ich sah, **wie** er die Straße überquerte.* |
| *Did you notice him **steal** the bag?*<br>→ *Haben Sie gesehen, **dass** er die Tasche stahl?* | *Did you notice him **stealing** the bag?*<br>→ *Haben Sie gesehen, **wie** er die Tasche stahl?* |
| Hier wird die **Tatsache, dass etwas geschah** betont. | Hier wird der **Verlauf der Handlung** betont. |

**34** Im Englischen unterscheidet man zwei Infinitiv-Arten, nämlich den

________________ und den ________________.

**35** Nach ________________ und deren Steigerungsformen steht der

________________.

**36** Der *to*-Infinitiv Passiv Präsens des Verbs *read* lautet ________________.

**37** *Ich weiß nicht, mit wem ich telefonieren soll* kann ins Englische mit Infinitiv

folgendermaßen übersetzt werden: ________________

________________.

**38** Ein Beispiel für den *to*-Infinitiv nach *somebody* ist: ________________.

**39** Übersetze die folgenden Sätze:
a) My brother wanted to leave his girlfriend.
b) My brother wanted his girlfriend to leave.
c) My brother made his girlfriend leave.
d) My brother had left his girlfriend.

________________

________________

________________

________________

**40** *Bare infinitives* kommen in folgenden Fällen vor:

________________

________________

**1** Finde den Fehler und verbessere ihn in der Leerzeile. ___/4

a) The police made the thief to open his bag.

______________________________

b) Robert ought have breakfast at the moment.

______________________________

c) Susan was wondering whether read the newspaper or watch TV.

______________________________

d) He was the first man land on the Moon.

______________________________

**2** Setze *to*-Infinitive im Aktiv oder im Passiv ein. ___/4

a) Every Sunday in the afternoon, Uncle Billy is the first ______________ (ask) for a piece of strawberry cake.

b) This car ought ______________ (bring back) to the car park now.

c) There's still a lot of work ______________ (do) by tomorrow.

d) It will be rather hard for her ______________ (smile) because she isn't going to win the beauty contest.

e) Why not ______________ (have) a nice dinner in one of the Italian restaurants?

**3** Übersetze und schreibe in dein Heft. ___/12

a) Es war die Nachricht über den Tod ihres Vaters, die sie veranlasste, sofort nach New York zu fliegen.
b) Dort bot ihr ihr Bruder an, in seinem Haus einige Tage lang zu wohnen.
c) Die Beerdigung eines Familienangehörigen ist das Schlimmste, das man sich vorstellen kann.
d) Jeder erwartete von ihr eine Trauerrede *(funeral ovation)* zu halten.
e) In der Kirche wusste sie nicht (mehr), ob sie weinen oder ihren Bruder trösten sollte.
f) Nach drei Tagen in New York war sie zu erschöpft, um gleich wieder nach Hause zurückzukehren.

**Gesamtpunktzahl**
___/20

# 7 Adverbs and adverbial phrases: Adverbien und Adverbialsätze

**Adjektive und Adverbien haben im Deutschen meist die gleiche Form, nicht aber im Englischen. Es ist daher nicht immer einfach für uns zu wissen, welche Form wir im Englischen wann verwenden müssen.**

## 7.1 Adverb und Adjektiv

Regel

**Adverb und Adjektiv – Funktion und Bildung**

**Adverbien und Adjektive** haben unterschiedliche Funktionen: **Adjektive** geben Auskunft darüber, **wie etwas ist**, d.h. sie beschreiben Nomen näher. **Adverbien** zeigen an, unter **welchen Umständen eine Handlung abläuft** (daher im Deutschen **Umstandswörter**). Sie beschreiben Verben, Adjektive, andere Adverbien und sogar ganze Sätze näher.

Die meisten Adverbien werden dadurch gebildet, dass man die Endsilbe *-ly* an ein Adjektiv anhängt, d.h aus ***near*** wird ***nearly*** aus ***quick*** wird ***quickly***.

| Adjektiv | Adverb | Adjektiv-Endung | Adverb-Endung |
|---|---|---|---|
| *angry* | → *angrily* | *-y* | → *-i(ly)* |
| *true* | → *truly* | stummes *-e* | → fällt weg → *-ly* |
| *terrific* | → *terrifically* | -ic | → *-ally* |
| *friendly* | → *in a friendly way* | -ly | Ersatzform: *in an* [adjective] *way/manner* |
| *good* | → *well* | | Das Adverb von *good* ist *well*. |

**1** Adjektiv oder Adverb? Setze die richtige Form ein.

Ann is ______________ (nice) dressed. She is riding her ______________ (new) scooter to the lake and she is singing ______________ (happy). When she rides her scooter, she is always very ______________ (cautious) and she always wears her helmet. Her helmet is ______________ (red) so that people can see her ______________ (easy). At the moment she is driving very ______________ (slow) through Lake Street because there are many ______________ (careless) people. Now a woman is stepping

______________ (quick) into the street. She is talking ______________ (nervous) on her mobile. Ann ______________ (quick) puts on the brakes. The woman looks at her ____________________ (unfriendly) and walks on right into a bike. The man in the car behind Susan starts to laugh ____________________ (nasty).

Regel

**Adverbien mit Adjektivform**

**Adjektivformen** stehen, …

- nach Verben, die auf einen **Zustand** oder eine **Eigenschaft** hinweisen oder dem Deutschen ***werden*** entsprechen, also z. B. *be, grow, keep, become, seem, get, remain, go, stay, turn*: *He has grown* ***old****. She turned* ***pale****.* Aber: *She* ***quickly*** *turned pale.*
- nach Verben, die den **Klang**, das **Aussehen**, den **Geschmack** oder den **Geruch einer Sache** näher bestimmen *(verbs of perception*, z. B. *sound, taste, look, smell): This sounds good. This soup tastes wonderful.*

Tipp

**Unterscheide!**

*Your feet don't smell* ***good****!* → *Deine Füße riechen nicht* ***gut****.*
*The dog can smell* ***well****.* → *Der Hund kann* ***gut*** *riechen.*
Beschreiben Verben wie *look, taste* und *smell* eine **aktive Tätigkeit**, muss die Adverb-Form folgen.

Regel

**Besonderheiten**

Es gibt Adverbien, die die **gleiche Form wie das Adjektiv** haben, z. B.: *fast, long, low, early, daily, weekly, far, better, last, less, least.*
Beachte folgende Sonderformen und deren Bedeutung:

| **Adjektiv** | | **Adverb** | |
|---|---|---|---|
| *hard* | schwer, hart | *hardly* | kaum |
| *late* | spät | *lately* | kürzlich |
| *fair* | fair | *fairly* | ziemlich |
| *just* | gerade | *justly* | zu Recht |
| *pretty* | hübsch, ziemlich | *prettily* | hübsch |
| *high* | hoch | *highly* | höchst |
| *near* | nahe | *nearly* | fast, beinahe |
| *free* | umsonst | *freely* | freimütig |
| *close* | nahe | *closely* | genau |
| *dear* | teuer | *dearly* | herzlich |

**2** Setze die richtige Form ein.

Ann was rather ______________ (pretty) but today she looked ______________ ______________________ (pretty; strange). She had been on her way to school, when a lorry had passed her and ______________________ (near) pushed her off her scooter. Usually she is very ______________________ (calm), but she had become very ______________________ (excited) because the driver had ______________ (simple) driven away. A man had stopped next to her and she said to him ______________________ and in a ______________ voice, "Why didn't he drive more ______________________? I could have fallen off and been ______________, if I hadn't watched out!" (angry; shrill; careful; dead)

Regel

### Die Stellung der Adverbien

- **Front position**
  Am **Anfang des Satzes** stehen Adverbien, die den **ganzen Satz** näher beschreiben, z.B. *Fortunately, …. Luckily ….*
  Am **Anfang des Satzes** stehen **Adverbien des Ortes und der Zeit** *(adverbs of place, adverbs of time)*, wenn sie **betont** sind oder um zu lange Gruppen am Ende zu vermeiden, z.B. *Tomorrow …. Every now and then, ….*
- **Mid position**
  **Vor dem Hauptverb**, bzw. **nach dem ersten Hilfsverb** stehen **Häufigkeitsadverbien** *(adverbs of frequency*, z.B. *ever, never, always*) und **Gradadverbien** (*adverbs of degree*, z.B. *fully, hardly*):
  *I've always known this. He often walks home. You hardly know anything. He should fully understand.*

  Dies gilt auch für **Adverbien der Art und Weise** *(adverbs of manner)*:
  *The director clearly analyzed the data.*
- **End position**
  **Nach dem Verb**, aber nie zwischen Verb und direktem Objekt stehen:
  Adverbien der **Art und Weise**, wenn diese nicht in *mid position* stehen *(The director analyzed the data clearly.)*, Adverbien des **Ortes** *(He lost his way in town.)*, Adverbien der **Zeit** (*He lost his way yesterday.*) und Adverbien der **bestimmten Häufigkeit**, z.B. *once, three times* (*He played the game twice.*).

Tipp

**Mehrere Adverbien – aber wohin?**

Stehen mehrere Adverbien am Ende eines Satzes, so gilt die Regel **A-O-Z**:

| Art und Weise | Ort | | Zeit | |
|---|---|---|---|---|
| | Richtung | Ort | genauer | allgemein |

Adverbien der bestimmten Häufigkeit findet man im Allgemeinen hinter den Ortsadverbien, aber vor den Zeitadverbien.
Um Adverbialhäufchen am Satzende zu vermeiden, versucht man am besten die „Unterbringung" in *front position* und *mid position*.

Die Position der Adverbien kann man sich auch mit einem möglichst kuriosen Satz merken, etwa: *Yesterday the train arrived quietly from London in the kitchen at 9 o'clock at night.*

**3** Bringe die Wörter in die richtige Reihenfolge. (Hefteintrag)

a) in London – Harry – always – in the bookstore – meets – Ron.
b) goes – today – he – into the magic shop – with Hermione.
c) a present – want to buy – at Abbot's – they – for Ron.
d) always – Ron – from his mum – gets – ugly sweaters.
e) leaves – the Hogwarts Express – from platform 9¾ – at eleven o'clock.

Regel

**Adverbial clauses**

Hauptsätze werden oft durch einen oder mehrere Nebensätze ergänzt. Ein **Nebensatz** (auch Gliedsatz, *clause*) ist ein unselbständiger, untergeordneter Satz, der mit einem Hauptsatz zusammengeschlossen werden muss. Nebensätze werden durch unterschiedliche Partikel, z. B. Konjunktionen oder Relativpronomen eingeleitet.

**4** Unterstreiche die Nebensätze.

a) After Susan had left the house, Tom started to clean the kitchen.
b) She couldn't do it because she had sprained her ankle.
c) He wanted to help her because their holidays were coming nearer and nearer.
d) Although he had better things to do, he didn't stop until he was finished.
e) If she doesn't improve, we will have to cancel our trip to New York.

## 7.2 Adverbiale Nebensätze

Regel

**Einleitende Partikel in unterschiedlichen adverbialen Nebensätzen**

- **Nebensätze der Zeit:**
  *after* - nachdem; *before* - bevor; *till/until* - bis; *as* - als, während; *now* (*that*) - (nun) da/wo; *as soon as* - sobald; *when* - als, (immer) wenn; *once* - sobald; *whenever* - wann (auch) immer, immer wenn; *while* - während; *since* - seit(dem); *as long as* - solange
- **Nebensätze des Orts und der Richtung:**
  *where* - wo, wohin; *wherever* - wo, wohin (auch immer)
- **Nebensätze des Grundes:**
  *because* - weil; *as, since* - da
- **Nebensätze der Bedingung:**
  *if* - wenn, falls; *unless* - sofern nicht, außer wenn, es sei denn, dass; *as long as* - sofern, solange; *in case (that)* - im Falle dass; *provided/providing that* - vorausgesetzt, dass; *on condition that* - unter der Bedingung, dass; *supposing (that)* - angenommen, dass
- **Nebensätze der Einräumung:**
  *although/though* - obwohl; *while* - obwohl; *when* - wo .... doch, obwohl; *even/even though* - selbst wenn; *if* - wenn ... auch
- **Nebensätze des Gegensatzes:**
  *whereas/while* - während
- **Nebensätze des Zwecks:**
  *in order that/so that, so;* - damit; *lest* (mit *should* ) - damit nicht
- **Nebensätze der Folge:**
  *so that* - so dass; *so/such ... that* - so/solche ... dass
- **Nebensätze des Vergleichs (clauses of comparison):**
  *as (so)* - wie; *as though/as if* - als ob

**5** Ordne die Nebensätze der richtigen Kategorie zu.

| | Beispielsatz | Nebensatz der/des |
|---|---|---|
| a) | As he was always late ... | ______________ |
| b) | Before you slip into unconsciousness ... | ______________ |
| c) | If I were a carpenter ... | ______________ |
| d) | ... even though he had been treating her badly. | ______________ |
| e) | ... wherever you will be hiding. | ______________ |

## 6 Verbinde die Sätze mithilfe einer Konjunktion.

a) Mike was late. He had overslept.

______________________________

b) I didn't like her present. I thanked her.

______________________________

c) I'll get up early on the day after the party. My parents won't see the mess.

______________________________

______________________________

d) I am hungry. I'll get myself a hamburger.

______________________________

## Training plus

**41** Bilde die Adverbien.

a) unfriendly ____________ b) basic ____________

c) hard ____________ d) quick ____________

**42** Bessere die Fehler aus.

a) He left quickly the room. ____________

b) The driver stopped quickly at 11 o'clock in front of the station.

______________________________

**43** Wann wird der Haupt- vom Nebensatz mit einem Komma abgetrennt?

______________________________

**44** In welchen drei Positionen können Adverbien auftreten?

______________________________

**45** Wie lautet die allgemeine Regel für die Stellung mehrerer Adverbien am Ende eines Satzes?

______________________________

___/10 **1** Setze die Adverbien/Adverbialen in die richtige Gruppe.

silently • angrily • at the end of the corridor • hard • in ancient times • fast • next to this old tower • lately • into the house • yesterday • already • pretty • often • slowly • behind the painting • very • long • for a few weeks • carefully • stupidly

**manner:** ______________________________

______________________________

**place:** ______________________________

______________________________

**time:** ______________________________

______________________________

**frequency:** ______________________________

______________________________

**degree:** ______________________________

______________________________

___/12 **2** Adjektiv oder Adverb?

Mr Miller was ______________ (deep) upset. He had bought a new camper and there were problems ______________ (near) everywhere. ______________ (just) as he wanted to go on holiday the engine sounded ______________ (rather, bad). He was ______________ (lucky) that he was not too ______________ (far) from the car dealer where he had bought it. He ______________ (slow) drove his car onto the forecourt and went into the show room. A young woman asked (polite) ______________ "What can I do for you?" and smiled ______________ (pretty). Mr Miller became ______________ (very, angry) and shouted, "If you don't repair my car for ______________ (free), I will put up a tent outside and tell everybody about it (relentless) ______________!" The young woman looked rather

________________ (shocked). Then a ________________ (nice), middle-aged man came ________________ (quick) out of an office. "Haven't I seen you here ________________ (late)?", he asked. Mr Miller turned ________________ (red) and said, "The car you sold me makes ________________ (terrible) sounds. The engine ________________ (hard) ever starts and the inside smells ________________ ________________ (extreme, bad)!"
"Why don't you keep ________________ (calm)?" stated the ________________ (smart), middle-aged man. "Let's see, what we can do! But you shouldn't talk about us ________________ (unfair)!"

**3** Verbinde die Sätze sinnvoll. ___/12

a) I didn't like the food. I ate it.

________________________________________

b) He forgot his wallet. He had paid at the restaurant.

________________________________________

c) She started to cry. He had left her.

________________________________________

d) The young couple's car left. The bride threw her flowers in the air.

________________________________________

**Gesamtpunktzahl ___/34**

# 8 Conditional forms and sentences: das Konditional und die Bedingungssätze

**Die Verwendung von Konditionalkonstruktionen und von Konditionalsätzen *(conditional sentences)* bereitet Schülerinnen und Schülern bis hinauf in die Oberstufe seltsamerweise immer wieder Probleme.**
**Hält man sich jedoch an wenige, dazu noch recht gut einprägsame Regeln, so kann man auf diesem Gebiet auf recht einfache Weise einen Großteil möglicher Fehlerquellen ausschalten.**

## 8.1 *Conditional I* und *Conditional II (Conditional Perfect)*

***Conditional I und II*** sind keine *tenses*. Sie können aber hinsichtlich ihrer Bildung mit dem *future* und dem *future perfect* verglichen werden, nur, dass an Stelle des *will* ein *would* (bzw. in der modalen Form ein *could/should*) steht.

Regel

***Conditional I***

Das ***conditional I*** drückt eine **Möglichkeit/Wahrscheinlichkeit** oder eine **persönliche Einstellung** aus:
*This would be disgusting.* → Das wäre abscheulich.
*I would not try to solve the problem right now.* → Ich würde nicht versuchen, das Problem sofort zu lösen.

***Would*** in Verbindung mit **Verben des Mögens** (z. B. *like, love*) drückt aus, dass man etwas (jetzt) gerne tun würde:
*I would like to have a cup of coffee now.* → Ich hätte jetzt gerne (statt: würde gerne haben) eine Tasse Kaffee. *He'd love to go swimming.* Er würde gerne schwimmen gehen.

**1** Bilde aus den Fragmenten Sätze im *conditional I*. (Hefteintrag)

a) She - not work - on Sundays.

b) The United Nations - never - work - against - international cooperation.

c) UNICEF - like to - narrow - the gap between starvation and survival.

d) The organization - love to - give children the right to grow up in health and peace.

Info plus

**UNICEF (United Nations International Children's Emergency Fund)**

Das Kinderhilfswerk der Vereinten Nationen mit Sitz in New York wurde im Jahr 1946 gegründet um Kindern in Europa nach den schrecklichen Erlebnissen des Zweiten Weltkriegs zu helfen. Heute arbeitet UNICEF mit etwa 8000 Mitarbeitern für die Kinder in 160 Staaten, vor allem in den Entwicklungsländern in den Bereichen Ernährung, Hygiene, Gesundheit und Bildung. Neben täglicher Routinearbeit kümmert sich die Organisation auch um humanitäre Unterstützung von Kindern in Notsituationen, so etwa während Hungersnöten, Bürgerkriegen und bei Naturkatastrophen. UNICEF setzt sich außerdem für den Schutz von Flüchtlingen und gegen den Einsatz von Kindersoldaten ein.

## 2 Übersetze in deinem Heft.

a) Ich würde das Angebot annehmen.

b) Hättest du gerne eine Königsfamilie in Deutschland?

c) Wärst du gerne reich oder würdest du lieber glücklich sein?

d) Würde er sagen, dieser Kandidat ist am besten für diese Position geeignet?

e) Das würde ich mir noch einmal überlegen.

Regel

***Conditional II***

Das ***conditional II*** drückt aus, dass man etwas gemacht hätte oder dass etwas eingetreten wäre: *I would have come to a different decision.* → Ich hätte anders entschieden. *He would have been happy.* → Er wäre glücklich gewesen.

Die Bildung des *conditional II (conditional perfect)* ist recht einfach: ***would*** (oder modal auch *could/should*) **+ *have* + Perfekt-Form des Verbs** (bei unregelmäßigen Verben also die dritte zu lernende Form des Verbs):
*She would have answered this question correctly. She should have known the answer to this question.*

Konditionalformen spielen besonders in Bedingungssätzen eine wichtige Rolle. Diese Sätze werden in den nachfolgenden Unterabschnitten genauer behandelt.

## 3 Forme die Sätze in das *conditional II* um. (Hefteintrag)

a) She would be happy to meet Sir Peter Ustinov, a UNICEF Goodwill Ambassador.

b) The man who first climbed Mount Everest without artificial oxygen would love to meet Sir Edmund Hillary.

c) The winning basketball team would love to be invited by the host team after the match.

d) A great deal of famine in the world could be eradicated.

e) Building a protective environment for our children should be a main goal in our life.

## 8.2 *Conditional sentences:* Konditional- oder Bedingungssätze

Regel

**Konditional- oder Bedingungssätze**

Im Englischen gibt es drei verschiedene Typen an Konditionalsätzen (Typ I, II und III). Sie alle sind an Bedingungen erfüllt, die entweder ziemlich sicher (Typ I), vielleicht (Typ II) oder gar nicht mehr (Typ III) erfüllt werden können. Das wohl wichtigste Wort in einem Konditionalsatz ist ***if***. Es bedeutet deutsch **wenn** im Sinne von *unter der Bedingung, dass ….*

**Typ I** wird verwendet, wenn der Sprecher glaubt, dass die Bedingung mit größerer Wahrscheinlichkeit erfüllt werden kann:

| ***if*-clause** (Nebensatz mit *if*) | ***main clause*** (Hauptsatz) |
| --- | --- |
| *If we don't speed up,*<br>Wenn wir nicht schneller fahren, | *… we will miss our plane.*<br>… werden wir unser Flugzeug verpassen. |
| ***present tense*** | ***will-Future*** |

**4** Übersetze in deinem Heft die Konditionalsätze (Typ I).

a) Wenn er sich wirklich für ein Medizinstudium interessiert, werden wir ihm nicht im Weg stehen.

b) Wenn du dieses alte Pferd wirklich kaufen wirst, (dann) musst du es gut pflegen.

c) Ich verlasse ihn, wenn er das tut.

d) Sogar wenn es stimmt, was du sagst, werde ich meine Meinung nicht ändern.

e) Wenn wir diese Buchung bestätigen, werden wir im Sommer nach Norwegen reisen.

**5** Bilde Konditionalsätze vom Typ I. (Hefteintrag)

| Bedingung | Folge |
|---|---|
| a) she/come | I/be/happy |
| b) US government/introduce/new/taxation | most Americans/support/it |
| c) you/google/this word | you/get/a lot of information/about/jazz |
| d) this quality newspaper/show/too many photos | it/risk/its reputation |

Tipp

**Ganz stur vorgehen und kein *if* im Hauptsatz!**

Verwende in den Konditionalsätzen immer ganz stur die vorgeschriebenen Verbformen, lasse dich dabei nicht durch eventuell abweichende Zeitformen im Deutschen beeinflussen. Entscheide immer nach dem Grad der Erfüllbarkeit der Bedingung. Und vergiss nie: ***If*** darf **nie im Hauptsatz**, sondern eben immer nur im Nebensatz auftauchen!

Regel

**Konditionalsatz Typ II**

Ein **Konditionalsatz vom Typ II** wird verwendet, wenn der Sprecher glaubt, dass die Bedingung mit größerer Wahrscheinlichkeit **eher nicht oder mit einer geringeren Wahrscheinlichkeit** erfüllt werden kann:

| ***if-clause***<br>(Nebensatz mit *if*) | ***main clause***<br>(Hauptsatz) |
|---|---|
| *If he worked constantly,*<br>Wenn er beständiger arbeitete, | *... he would pass his exam.*<br>... würde er sein Examen bestehen. |
| Die Wahrscheinlichkeit, dass er sein Examen besteht, ist hier deutlich gering, da er ja nicht beständig arbeitet. | |
| ***past tense*** | ***conditional I*** |

**6** Bilde Konditionalsätze vom Typ II. Verwende die Angaben aus Übung 5 und schreibe in dein Heft.

**7** Übersetze in deinem Heft.

a) Wenn der Präsidentschaftskandidat der Demokraten diese Wahl gewänne, wären die Republikaner tief enttäuscht.

b) Solltest du ihm dieses Geheimnis verraten, wäre ich ziemlich wütend.

c) Das Layout dieser Seite wäre ansprechender, würde man eine andere Schriftart (*typeface*) verwenden.

d) Wenn der internationale Gerichtshof diesen Kriegsverbrecher schuldig spräche, wären tausende Flüchtlingsopfer des Krieges zufriedengestellt.

Regel

**Konditionalsatz Typ III**

Ein **Konditionalsatz vom Typ III** wird verwendet, wenn der Sprecher ausdrücken will, was passiert wäre, wenn die Bedingung erfüllt worden wäre. Das Ganze dreht sich also um den Spruch „Wenn das Wörtchen „wenn" nicht wäre…", denn die Bedingung liegt in der Vergangenheit und nichts ist mehr zu ändern.

| ***if*-clause**<br>(Nebensatz mit *if*) | ***main clause***<br>(Hauptsatz) |
|---|---|
| *If you had told me the story,*<br>Wenn du mir die Geschichte erzählt hättest, | *I would have been relieved.*<br>wäre ich erleichtert gewesen. |
| ***past perfect*** | ***conditional II*** |

**8** Bilde Konditionalsätze vom Typ III. Verwende die Angaben aus Übung 5 und schreibe in dein Heft.

**9** Übersetze in deinem Heft.

a) Wenn ich das gewusst hätte, hätte ich niemals zugestimmt.

b) Hättest du dieses Problem lösen können, (dann) hättest du nicht noch einmal mit der ganzen Gruppe sprechen müssen.

c) Wenn wir am bilingualen Unterricht teilgenommen hätten, wären wir in der Lage gewesen, diesen geografischen Text ins Englische zu übersetzen.

d) Wenn ich noch einmal den falschen PIN-Code eingegeben hätte, (dann) hätte der Geldautomat meine Karte gesperrt.

e) Hätte er nicht einen so bezaubernden Charme gehabt, wären wir sicherlich nicht auf ihn reingefallen.

f) Was wäre geschehen, wenn sie den Zug verpasst hätte?

g) Hätte er mir auf der Fähre nach Hull nicht ständig Geschichten über Schiffsunglücke erzählt, wäre ich sicherlich besser gelaunt gewesen.

Regel

## Ausnahmen bei Konditionalsätzen

- **Typ I**: ***Simple present*** in *if-clause* **und** *main clause*: Wenn der Sprechende ausdrücken will, dass etwas **Allgemeingültigkeit** hat oder **immer wieder so geschieht**, dann wird das ***simple present*** in Haupt- **und** Nebensatz verwendet. *if* steht dann in der Bedeutung von „Immer wenn …" *(Whenever …)*:
  *If you heat ice, it melts. If you don't have lunch now, you get hungry later.*
- **Typ III**: *Past perfect* im *if*-Satz, aber ***conditional I*** *(would/wouldn't + infinitive)* **im Hauptsatz**: Wenn der Sprechende ausdrücken will, wie eine Situation in der Gegenwart wäre, wenn etwas in der Vergangenheit anders gelaufen wäre, dann setzt man ***conditional I* im Hauptsatz**:
  *If I had talked to him, I wouldn't be angry now.*

**10** Übersetze die folgenden, von den üblichen Mustern der Typen I – III abweichenden Sätze. Schreibe in dein Heft.

a) Wenn du kleiner schreibst, passt mehr auf diese Seite.

______________________________

______________________________

b) Wenn wir den anderen Weg gegangen wären, säßen wir jetzt schon auf der Terrasse unseres Hotels in der Sonne.

______________________________

______________________________

c) Immer wenn sie kommt, freue ich mich.

______________________________

46 Wie wird das *conditional I* gebildet? ______________________________

______________________________

47 Wie wird das *conditional II* gebildet? ______________________________

______________________________

48 Wo darf *would* in der Regel nicht auftauchen?

______________________________

49 Ist die Bedingung im Konditionalsatz vom Typ III erfüllbar?

______________________________

50 Welche *tenses* tauchen im Konditionalsatz vom Typ III auf?

Hauptsatz: ______________________________

Nebensatz: ______________________________

51 Was darf nie im Hauptsatz eines Konditionalsatzes stehen? ______________

52 In welchem Konditionalsatztyp kann ein *past perfect* auftreten? Typ ________

53 In welchem Konditionalsatztyp kann ein *will-Futur* auftreten? Typ ________

54 Unter welchen Umständen kann in Haupt- und Nebensatz eines Konditionalsatzes das *simple present* auftreten?

______________________________

______________________________

**1** Setze die folgenden Sprechabsichten in entsprechende Konditionalsätze um, schreibe in dein Heft. ___/12

a) Du hast das Tennismatch nicht gewonnen. Du hättest einen Sieg gefeiert.
b) Du machst einen Versuch und stellst fest: Immer wenn du den Plastikstab reibst, entsteht elektrische Spannung.
c) Du würdest dich sehr über eine Verlängerung des Vertrags eines Spielers bei der gegnerischen Mannschaft ärgern.
d) Du stellst deinen Partner auf die Probe: Wenn er noch einmal solchen Unsinn über dich erzählt, wirst du Konsequenzen ergreifen.
e) Du stellst fest: Hätte man über die Probleme rechtzeitig gesprochen, dann würde man sich jetzt nicht mit dem Konkurs *(bankruptcy)* abfinden müssen.
f) Du beklagst dich darüber, dass der Brief nicht aufgegeben wurde und die Reise deshalb nicht gebucht werden konnte.

**2** Kreuze den Konditionalsatz-Typ anhand der gegebenen Fragmente an. ___/8

| | Fragment | I | II | III |
|---|---|---|---|---|
| a) | If she had tidied up her room, … | ☐ | ☐ | ☐ |
| b) | … my father wouldn't have discussed it over and over. | ☐ | ☐ | ☐ |
| c) | If the plan is carried out, … | ☐ | ☐ | ☐ |
| d) | If she knew about his escapades, … | ☐ | ☐ | ☐ |
| e) | … the party would get rid of the three illoyal members. | ☐ | ☐ | ☐ |
| f) | … America wouldn't have been discovered in 1492. | ☐ | ☐ | ☐ |
| g) | If President Obama brought back the troops from Iraq, … | ☐ | ☐ | ☐ |
| h) | … the new zoo in Belfast will be erected in time. | ☐ | ☐ | ☐ |

**3** Finde den Fehler und korrigiere den entsprechenden Teilsatz. ___/5

a) If she eats chocolate, she would become nervous and excited.

___________________________________________

b) If you would have used this pronoun, the sentence would have been correct.

___________________________________________

c) If all people on our planet cared about environment, we will live in a better world.

___________________________________________

d) She'll be one of the finalists, if she won this match.

___________________________________________

e) Whenever you shake the tree, the apples would come down.

___________________________________________

**Gesamtpunktzahl** ___/25

# 9 *Relative sentences:* Relativsätze

**Relativsätze bestehen aus einem Hauptsatz *(main clause)* und einem Nebensatz *(relative clause)*. Im Nebensatz wird ein Element, z. B. eine Person oder eine Sache, genauer erläutert oder bestimmt, sodass der gesamte Satz erst dann einen Sinn ergibt.**

## 9.1 *Defining relative clauses*

Regel

***Defining relative clauses*** **– notwendige Relativnebensätze**

- **Notwendige Relativnebensätze** *(defining relative clauses)* beschreiben, erläutern oder geben Informationen über Personen oder Dinge des Hauptsatzes so, dass erst mit ihrer Hilfe der Gesamtsatz (bestehend aus Haupt- und Nebensatz) Sinn ergibt. In diesen Sätzen werden Haupt- und Nebensatz im Gegensatz zum Deutschen im Englischen **nicht mit einem Komma abgetrennt**:
  *The man who lives next to me is 70 years old.* → Der Satz *The man is 70 years old* würde isoliert stehend keinen Sinn ergeben, weil man nicht wüsste, welcher Mann gemeint ist.

**Relativpronomen in notwendigen *(defining)* Relativsätzen**

- **Bezug auf Personen**
  Bei einem Bezug auf eine oder mehrere Personen verwendet man das Relativpronomen ***who***, wenn dieses sich auf eine oder mehrere Personen im Subjekt- oder Objektfall bezieht:
  **Subjekt-Bezug:** *The young lady who is standing next to Paula is my sister Anne.*
  **Objekt-Bezug:** *The young lady who I met yesterday is my English teacher.*

  Bezieht sich das im Nebensatz Gesagte auf **eine oder mehrere Personen** im Sinne von deutsch *dessen* oder *deren*, so verwendet man das Relativpronomen ***whose***: *The pupil whose schoolbag was stolen last week is 14.*

- **Bezug auf Dinge und Tiere**
  Man verwendet das Relativpronomen ***which***, wenn dieses sich auf **eine oder mehrere Dinge/Tiere im Subjekt- oder Objektfall** bezieht:
  **Subjekt-Bezug:** *This is a CD which has some really good tracks.*
  **Objekt-Bezug:** *Yesterday John watched the cat which he had fed some days ago.*

  Bezieht sich das im Nebensatz Gesagte auf **ein oder mehrere Dinge/Tiere** im Sinne von deutsch *dessen* oder *deren*, so verwendet man die Konstruktion ***of which***: *We soon noticed the problem the solution of which was rather difficult.*

- Das Relativpronomen ***that*** kann sowohl **für Personen als auch für Dinge/Tiere bei Subjekt- oder Objektbezug** verwendet werden: *This is a CD that has some really good tracks. The young lady that is standing next to Paula is my sister Anne.*

## 1 Entscheide, ob die Sätze notwendige Relativsätze sind. Kreuze an.

| | notwendig | nicht notwendig |
|---|---|---|
| a) Der Mann, der neben dir steht, ist blond. | ☐ | ☐ |
| b) Paula, die Sängerin ist, sieht sehr hübsch aus. | ☐ | ☐ |
| c) Bill hat ein Fahrrad, dessen Farbe blau ist. | ☐ | ☐ |
| d) Ein Architekt ist jemand, der Häuser entwirft. | ☐ | ☐ |
| e) Ich verlor den Schlüssel, den sie mir gab. | ☐ | ☐ |

## 2 Bilde notwendige Relativsätze. Verwende ein Relativpronomen und schreibe in Klammern mögliche andere Relativpronomen.

a) Sally is talking to the girl ______________________________ she argued with.

b) I love the Celtic song ______________________________ I heard yesterday.

c) The old lady ______________________________ house is near by the river has died.

d) The new TV spot ______________________________ presents the XXL sports car is something ______________________________ I don't like very much

## 3 Übersetze in deinem Heft.

a) Robert telefoniert gerade mit dem Mädchen, das ihn vor einigen Stunden auf dem Schulhof angesprochen hat.

b) Ich glaube, ich kenne den Film, dessen Titel ich leider vergessen habe.

c) Kannst du mir den Namen der jungen Dame nennen, deren Bruder mit mir im Judoclub trainiert?

Regel

### *Contact clauses*

***Contact clauses*** sind ganz besondere Relativsätze. Wenn das Relativpronomen in einem notwendigen Relativsatz das **Objekt des Nebensatzes** ist, kann man es weg lassen. Die folgenden drei Sätze wurden also alle richtig gebildet:

- Relativpronomen ***who***: *I know the man **who** I saw yesterday.*
- Relativpronomen ***that***: *I know the man **that** I saw yesterday.*
- **kein** Relativpronomen: *I know the man I saw yesterday.*

Gleiches gilt analog bei Dingen/Tieren:
*I like the cottage **which** (oder **that** oder –) I saw yesterday.*

**4** Mache ein Kreuz hinter jeden Satz, aus dem man einen *contact clause* machen kann.

a) Are you seriously planning to go on the Everest tour that the new travel agency is offering? ☐

b) The name of the man who first climbed the highest mountain was Hillary, wasn't it? ☐

c) The team almost died when they tried to get to the summit of the mountain which was also called Chomolungma. ☐

**Info plus**

### Der Mount Everest

Der Mount Everest (tibetisch: Chomolungma) ist der höchste Berg der Erde mit einer Höhe von 8848 Metern. Er liegt im Khumbu-Himalaya-Gebiet in Nepal an der Grenze zu China. Letztendlich entstand der Berg infolge plattentektonischer Vorgänge, bei denen sich Indien - vor zig Millionen Jahren noch ein Inselkontinent - in die eurasiatische Platte hineinschob und somit ein riesiges Faltengebirge hochwölben ließ. Das Himalaya-Gebirge ist somit nichts anderes als das Ergebnis eines gewaltigen geologischen „Auffahrunfalls".

Der Berg wurde nach dem britischen Landvermesser Sir George Everest benannt. Im Jahre 1953 bestiegen der Neuseeländer Edmund Hillary und der Sherpa Tenzing Norgay zum ersten Mal den Berg unter Zuhilfenahme von künstlichem Sauerstoff, denn die Dichte der Luft in der sogenannten Todeszone ab 8000 m entspricht etwa nur noch einem Drittel der an der Erdoberfläche auf Meereshöhe.

**Regel**

### Präpositionen in *contact clauses*

Wenn das Verb in einem *contact clause* eine **Präposition** bei sich hat (z.B. *listen to, think of, talk about*), dann stellt man die Präposition an das **Ende des *contact clause***:
*She doesn't like talking about the music which (that/-) her brother is listening to. Ah, there's the copy of the mp3 file which (that/-) I told you about.*

**5** Übersetze in deinem Heft. Bilde *contact clauses* (ohne Relativpronomen) und achte auf die Position auftretender Präpositionen.

a) Eva streitet gerade mit der Frau, mit der sie gestern gesprochen hatte.

b) Das Dokument, das du ausgefüllt hast, kam nie bei mir an.

c) Das Buch, nach welchem du gerade suchst, ist in meinem Regal.

## 9.2 Non-defining relative clauses

Regel

***Non-defining relative clauses*** **– nicht notwendige Relativnebensätze**

**Nicht notwendige Relativnebensätze *(non-defining relative clauses)*** beinhalten **zusätzliche Informationen**, die jedoch **nicht notwendig** sind um den Hauptsatz eine sinnvolle Aussage machen zu lassen. Solche Relativnebensätze stehen **immer zwischen Kommas**. Die zu verwendenden **Relativpronomen** lauten ***who*** (Bezug auf Personen), ***which*** (Bezug auf Dinge/Tiere) und ***whose***. Das Relativpronomen ***that*** darf in diesen Relativnebensätzen **nicht verwendet** werden. Außerdem können **keine *contact clauses*** gebildet werden.

**6** Bilde aus den zwei Einzelsätzen je einen *non-defining relative clause.* (Hefteintrag)

a) Mein älterer Bruder baut eine Modellrakete. Er ist Ingenieur.
b) Das alte Haus am Fluss wird gerade verkauft. Der Fluss heißt, glaube ich, Rio Caldo.
c) Die ältere Schwester meiner Tante ist meine Mutter. Der jüngere Bruder meiner Tante hat zwei Söhne.
d) Seit zwei Jahren arbeitet John in einer Kraftfahrzeugwerkstatt. Johns Bruder ist 16.

**7** Übersetze. Schreibe in dein Heft.

a) Rose, deren jüngerer Bruder in der Schule oft gemobbt *(to bully)* wird, will mit dem Direktor sprechen.
b) Der Freund meines Onkels, der sich gestern einen James-Bond-Film angesehen hatte, wurde heute während des Abendessens ohnmächtig.
c) Die Karikaturen in dieser Zeitschrift, die in Deutschland und Österreich verkauft wird, finde ich schrecklich.
d) Das achttägige Outdoorcamp, das von Schülern unserer Schule organisiert wurde, war ein voller Erfolg.
e) Paul, der 17-jährige Nachbarjunge, der in Atlanta geboren wurde, will ein Hochschulstipendium bekommen.

Tipp

***Which*** kann als Relativpronomen auch dann verwendet werden, wenn man die **gesamte** Aussage im Hauptsatz kommentieren oder bewerten will:
*The terraced house in our street was sold under price, which is really annoying.*
*Susan would like to take the morning ferry to Ireland, which seems to be a great idea.*

**8** Füge den zweiten Teil des folgenden Relativsatzes hinzu.

a) In order to compensate for the malfunction of the ship's spotlights, the fishermen made use of flashlights, __________________________________________________________________________________________.

( … was keine schlechte Idee war.)

b) The judge announced that he would sentence the accused immediately, ____________________________________________.

( … was, so glaube ich, das Beste war, das er tun konnte.)

c) My horoscope tells me that I might be lucky this week, ____________________________________________

( … was mir wirklich gefällt.)

## Training plus

**55** Welche Relativnebensätze stehen im Englischen immer zwischen Kommas?

____________________________________________

**56** Was ist ein *defining relative clause*? ____________________________________________

____________________________________________

**57** Welche Relativpronomen können für Personen im *defining relative clause*, welche für Personen im *non-defining relative clause* vorkommen?

*defining:* ____________________________________________

*non-defining:* ____________________________________________

**58** Unter welchen Bedingungen kann ein *contact clause* gebildet werden?

____________________________________________

**1** Bringe die folgenden Sprechabsichten mithilfe von Relativsatzkonstruktionen zum Ausdruck. Schreibe in dein Heft. ___/15

a) Teile deiner Freundin Sally mit, dass du dich sehr für die Sightseeing-Tour interessierst, über die du in dem Reisemagazin gelesen hast.
b) Frage Ken, wohin er den grässlichen Teppich gebracht hat, den er dir zu Weihnachten geschenkt hat.
c) Bekunde dein Missfallen über die Art und Weise, wie ein Problem gelöst werden soll.
d) Drücke aus, dass mehr als 40 Polizisten bei den Unruhen, die am Montag begannen, verletzt wurden.
e) Sage, dass du die Tatsache, dass mehrere Personen an der Vogelgrippe erkrankt sind, als beunruhigend empfindest.

**2** Streiche die nicht möglichen Relativpronomen durch. ___/5

a) I talked to the old lady which/that/who/whose car had broken down in front of the church.
b) Mrs. Dexter did not see the snake which/that/who/whose was approaching on the floor.
c) Sydney, that/who/whose/which is the largest city in Australia, is not the capital.
d) The World Wide Web, that/who/whose/which was invented by a US-American, has changed our life.
e) They're planning to build a new activity park down by the river, that/who/which I think is a great idea.

**3** Bilde aus den beiden deutschen Teilsätzen je einen englischen Relativsatz ___/6

a) Ich liebe italienisches Essen. Besonders liebe ich das italienische Essen, das in der Pizzeria an der Ecke serviert wird.

______________________________________________

______________________________________________

b) Er wird ein Angebot machen. Wir werden das Angebot nicht akzeptieren können.

______________________________________________

______________________________________________

c) Eine Giraffe ist ein Tier. Die Giraffe lebt in der Savanne.

______________________________________________

______________________________________________

**Gesamtpunktzahl** ___/26

# 10 *Reported Speech:* Indirekte Rede

**Viel öfter als man glaubt, muss man berichten, was jemand sagt, denkt, gesagt oder gedacht hat. Hierfür brauchen wir die indirekte Rede *(reported speech)*.**

## 10.1 Sag es indirekt!

Regel

**Die indirekte Rede – *reporting verb* in der Gegenwart**

Sätze in der indirekten Rede bestehen meist aus zwei Teilen, dem ***reporting clause*** und dem ***reported clause***. Der *reporting clause* zeigt an, dass etwas berichtet wird, der *reported clause* selbst berichtet über den Inhalt.

| reporting clause | reported clause |
|---|---|
| He says … | … that he hasn't had dinner yet. |
| She answered … | … that the dog had bitten the postman. |

Steht das ***reporting verb*** *(say, tell, explain …)* in der Gegenwart, werden im ***reported clause*** wie im Deutschen nur **Pronomen und Ortsangaben** (wo nötig) verändert, nicht aber die *tenses*. Manchmal müssen auch, genau wie im Deutschen, die Zeitangaben der Situation angepasst werden.

| direkte Rede *direct speech* | indirekte Rede *reported speech* |
|---|---|
| *I* | *he, she* |
| *you* | *he, she* |
| *we* | *they* |
| *you (plural)* | *they* |
| *my* | *his, her* |
| *here* | *there* |

| direkte Rede *direct speech* | indirekte Rede *reported speech* |
|---|---|
| *your* | *his, her* |
| *our* | *their* |
| *your (plural)* | *their* |
| *this* | *that* |
| *these* | *those* |

**1** Tim und Tom unterhalten sich im Moment. Sam steht dabei, aber er kann zur Zeit wegen einer Ohrenentzündung nicht gut hören. Deswegen fragt er Tim immer wieder danach, was Tom ihm (Tim) gerade erzählt. Verwende in der folgenden Übung *reporting verbs* im Präsens und bilde die richtigen *reported clauses.*

Tom (to Tim): "My computer doesn't work."
Sam (to Tim): "What does he say?"

Tim (to Sam): *"He says his computer doesn't work."*

a) Tom (to Tim): "My parents mustn't know about this!"
Sam (to Tim): "What does he say?"

Tim (to Sam): "He ________________________________________________."

b) Tom (to Tim): "I don't know how to solve this problem."
Sam (to Tim): "What does he say?"

Tim (to Sam): "He ________________________________________________."

c) Tom (to Tim): "The only thing I can do is repair it."
Sam (to Tim): "What does he say?"

Tim (to Sam): "He ________________________________________________."

Regel

### Die indirekte Rede – *reporting verb* in einer Vergangenheitsform

Steht das *reporting verb* in einer *tense* **der Vergangenheit**, werden nicht nur die oben stehenden Pronomen und Ortsangaben geändert, sondern es treten auch die Regeln der Zeitenfolge *(sequence of tenses)* in Kraft, das heißt die Zeiten müssen der Situation angepasst werden und eine **Stufe in die Vergangenheit zurückgeschoben**, sozusagen „gealtert" werden *(backshift)*. Auch Zeitangaben werden meist angepasst.

| **direkte Rede** ***direct speech*** | **indirekte Rede** ***reported speech*** | **direkte Rede** ***direct speech*** | **indirekte Rede** ***reported speech*** |
|---|---|---|---|
| *simple present* | *simple past* | *present progressive* | *past progressive* |
| *simple past* | *past perfect* | *past progressive* | *past perfect progressive* |
| *present perfect* | *past perfect* | *present perfect progressive* | *past perfect progressive* |
| *past perfect* | bleibt: *past perfect* | *past perfect pro-gressive* | bleibt: *past perfect progressive* |
| *will* | *would* | *am/are/is going to* | *was/were going to* |
| *today* | *that day (an jenem Tag)* | *yesterday* | *the day before* |
| *x days/weeks/ years ago* | *x days/weeks/ years before* | *last week/year* | *the week/year before* |
| *tomorrow* | *the next/ following day* | *next week/year* | *the following week/year* *a week/year later* |
| *now* | *then* | *This morning/ afternoon/evening/ night/month* | *that morning/ afternoon/evening/ night/month* |

**2** Tim und Tom unterhielten sich vorgestern. Tim berichtet Sam **heute**, was Tom ihm (Tim) vorgestern erzählte. Verwende in der Übung *reporting verbs* in der Vergangenheit. Bilde die richtigen *reported clauses*.

Tom (zu Tim, vorgestern): "My computer doesn't work."

Tim (zu Sam, heute): *He said his computer didn't work.*

a) Tom (zu Tim, vorgestern): "My parents mustn't know about this!"

Tim (zu Sam, heute): He ______________________________.

b) Tom (zu Tim, vorgestern): "I don't know how to solve this problem."

Tim (zu Sam, heute): He ______________________________.

c) Tom (zu Tim, vorgestern): "The only thing I can do is repair it."

Tim (zu Sam, heute): He ______________________________."

Regel

**(Modale) Hilfsverben in der indirekten Rede**

Die (modalen) Hilfsverben verändern sich in der indirekten Rede wie folgt:
*can → could; may → might; shall → should; will → would; could → could; might → might; should → should; ought to → ought to; would → would; must → had to /must; needn't → didn't have to/needn't do; mustn't → wasn't/ weren't allowed to/mustn't.*

**3** Bilde Sätze in der indirekten Rede.

a) "I can see nothing with these glasses."

*He says he* ______________________________

b) "She wasn't allowed to see him."

*He reported* ______________________________

c) "This can't be possible."

*She said* ______________________________

d) "I must tell you the truth."

*He said* ______________________________

Regel

***Reported questions***

- Bei ***reported questions*** gelten in der indirekten Rede die **gleichen Regeln wie in Aussagesätzen**: Je nach benutzter *tense* beim ***reporting verb***, muss die Zeit in der indirekten Frage angepasst werden. Auch die Pronomen werden wieder verändert, wenn es der Sinn des Satzes erfordert. Dies sind typische ***reporting verbs***: *ask, wonder (whether), want to know.*
- Bei **Fragen ohne Fragewort** steht in der indirekten Rede ein ***if*** oder ***whether*** (deutsch: *ob*): *John: „Do you practise any sports?"* → *John asked George if (whether) he practised any sports.*
- Bei **Fragen mit einem Fragewort** *(who, what, where, when, why, …)* wird das **Fragewort in die indirekte Frage mit eingebaut**: *John: "Why do you play football and where do you play it?"* → *John asked him **why** he played football and **where** he played it.*

**Merke:** *Reported questions* haben keine Fragezeichen. Die Wortstellung entspricht der Wortstellung eines **Aussagesatzes**. Fragen **müssen nicht** mit *do/does/did* umschrieben werden.

**4** Berichte folgenden Dialog. Schreibe in dein Heft.

Mike: Are you going to come now? We wanted to be at the party 30 minutes ago and I've been waiting here for nearly one hour.

Jay: Can't you be a little more patient? I had to wash my hair and I still don't know what trousers I will wear. You haven't really been much help, have you.

Mike: I simply can't understand it. You have been putting on trousers and T-shirts endlessly. Who do you want to impress?

Jay: It's not a matter of impressing somebody, it's a matter of style.

Mike: The last person I waited for so long was my ex-girlfriend. But you're even slower than her. And you're a boy! Are you finally finished?

Jay: I can't go now, I still have to dry my hair.

Mike: That's it, I'm leaving. See you at the party.

At the party Mike had to tell the people where he had been and what had happened. He starts like this:

*After I had been waiting for an hour I asked Jay …*

Info plus

### The Car Industry

Keine andere Technologie hat die USA mehr beeinflusst als das Auto. Und das Zentrum der Autoindustrie ist Detroit, das in den USA auch *Motor City* genannt wird. Es ist Sitz der sogenannten *Big Three*: General Motors, der Ford Motor Company aus dem benachbarten Ort Dearborn und Chrysler mit Sitz im nahegelegenen Auburn Hills. Auch der deutsche Volkswagen-Konzern ist im nördlichen Vorort Auburn Hills vertreten. Immer noch arbeiten ungefähr ein Viertel aller in der Automobilindustrie Beschäftigten in oder in der Umgebung von Detroit. In den letzten Jahren ist die Automobilindustrie in den USA in der Krise, die veraltete Technik der *gas guzzler* (Benzinsäufer) und die starke Konkurrenz aus Europa und Asien sorgten für stark sinkende Absatzzahlen und zum Teil mussten und müssen Firmen sogar Insolvenz anmelden.

Tipp

### *that, whether* und *weather*

In der Regel kann *that* auch weggelassen werden. Im Gegensatz zum deutschen *dass*, steht im Englischen vor *that* nie ein Komma, auch nicht in der indirekten Rede. Verwechsle *whether* (ob) nicht mit *weather* (Wetter) - ein häufiger Fehler!

**5** **Letztes Jahr verbrachte Valentin, ein Schüler aus Augsburg, ein Jahr in den USA, wo er eine *guided tour* im Henry Ford Museum in Detroit besuchte. Nach seiner Rückkehr möchte er eine Reportage für seine Schülerzeitung schreiben. Setze die gestellten Fragen in die direkte Rede.**

During the tour the guide said:
"Good afternoon ladies and gentlemen. I'm Larry, your tour guide. Before we get into the museum let me give you some general information. If you have any questions, feel free to ask.
Today it is virtually unimaginable that only about 100 years ago cars were unaffordable for the bigger part of the population. Henry Ford was the person to change that."

**Questions**: "Did Ford invent the car?" "Compared to today, how expensive were cars?"

"He did not invent the automobile.
When he started making his own cars in about 1900, automobiles cost so much that only rich people could afford them. The average worker would have had to work for nearly one year to be able to afford a cheap car. Ford thought that he could make plenty of money selling cars, if he was able to produce them cheaply enough."

**Questions**: "How could this be achieved?" "Did he invent new methods of production?"

"Ford knew that efficient manufacturing was the key to making less expensive cars. In Chicago, Ford had seen meat packers working in a line so he decided to try this assembly line method in his factory. He put his workers in a line along a conveyor belt and the auto travelled on the belt from person to person, and each worker added a part."

**Questions**: "How much time did they save by this new method?" "Did other car manufacturers react?

"Car-building time was cut from about 14 hours to only 1 hour 33 seconds. The assembly line became a standard feature in the manufacturing process not only in car-building, and the price of the Model T, or Tin Lizzie, dropped from $1200 to about $ 295 and so many people could afford it."

**Questions**: "Why was that so important? I mean, cars aren't really that necessary."

"Well, the fact that people could own a car allowed them to commute to the city more easily, which led to quicker growth of the suburbs. Cities became the place where people worked. But they lived in the green suburbs. Driving also made travelling easier for people. And drive-thrus and motels wouldn't exist without Henry Ford's invention."

**Question**: "But isn't high pollution and the destruction of our environment also a result of his changes?"

"Ah, I think we can go into the museum now! Thanks a lot for your attention."

Tipp

Orts- und Zeitangaben in der indirekten Rede verändern sich natürlich nur, wenn sich Zeit oder Ort, an dem etwas gesagt wird, auch ändern. Das gilt auch für die Pronomen.

Also:
Jack at 10 o'clock: *"My girlfriend left me last week."*
John to Mary: *"He says (that) his girlfriend left him last week."*
John to Mary two years later: *"Two years ago, Jack told me that his girlfriend had left him the week before."*

## 10.2 Noch mehr Indirektes

**Regel**

***suggestions, advice, commands, invitations and requests***

- ***Indirect suggestions* (indirekte Vorschläge)** kann man so ausdrücken:
  - *suggest* + Verb-*ing*: *Stephen **suggested going** to the movies.*
  - *suggest* + *that (s.b.) should* + Verb: *Mary **suggested that** they **should go** to a museum instead.*
- ***Indirect advice*** (indirekte Ratschläge) werden so gebildet:
  - *advise s.b. to do s.th.: He advised me to take an umbrella.*
- ***Indirect commands*** (indirekte Befehle): *command/order/tell s.b. to (not to) do s.th.: Stephen told Mary not to worry about being late. The police officer ordered me to stand still.*
- In ***indirect invitations*** (indirekten Einladungen) verwendet man die *reporting verbs invite/offer/ask s.b. (not) to do s.th.: Mary invited Stephen to have coffee first.* Die Konstruktion *invite/offer/ask s.b. if s.b. would (wouldn't) do s.th* ist ebenfalls möglich. Hier liegt kein *if*-Satz im eigentlichen Sinn vor. *Would* hat hier die Bedeutung von *wollen/gerne mögen.*: *Mary asked Stephen if he would have another cup of coffee.*
- In ***indirect requests*** (indirekten Bitten) kann man *ask/beg s.b. (not) to do s.th.* verwenden: *She asked me not to tell her father about the fact that she …*

**6** 20 Jahre nachdem Lin in die Wisteria Lane gezogen war, erinnert sie sich an ihr erstes Gespräch mit Chris. Übersetze. Suche aus dem folgenden Pool an reporting verbs passende heraus. Schreibe in dein Heft.

say • tell sb. (not) to • be of the opinion • suggest doing something • propose • shout • whisper • scream • admit • exclaim • promise • want to know • advise • offer • ask • answer • reply • explain • concede • complain • agree • remark • ask whether • wonder whether • invite

a) Ich wollte wissen, wie lange er schon in der Straße wohnte.
b) Er stellte fest, dass er schon von Geburt an dort lebte.
c) Meine Mutter fragte ihn, ob er einen Sport ausübe.
d) Chris antwortete, dass er seit 10 Jahren Fußball spiele und schon zweimal den Stadtwettbewerb gewonnen habe.
e) Dann riet ihm mein Vater nicht so viel vor dem Spielen zu essen, weil er sonst *(otherwise)* nicht so schnell rennen könne.
f) Ich schimpfte meinen Vater, dass er seine Nase nicht in die Angelegenheiten anderer Leute stecken *(to meddle with)* solle.
g) Dann wollte Chris wissen, ob wir schon gegessen hatten, und lud uns ein, mit seiner Familie zu grillen.

**59** Steht das *reporting verb* im Präsens, so findet kein ______________________ statt.

**60** Reporting verbs bei indirekten Befehlen sind z. B.:

a) ______________________

b) ______________________

c) ______________________

**61** Zeitangaben ändern sich nur dann, wenn ______________________

______________________.

**62** *Backshift* bedeutet, dass ______________________

______________________

**63** Die Zeitangabe *yesterday* der direkten Rede verändert sich nach *Last year he said* … in ______________________

______________________.

**64** *Reporting verbs* in *indirect invitations* sind z. B.:

______________________

______________________

**65** Will man in der indirekten Rede Vorschläge realisieren, dann verwendet man z. B.:

______________________

______________________

oder ______________________

______________________

__/30 **1** Du bist ein Reporter (eine Reporterin) für ein Jugendmagazin und interviewst den Sänger der Gruppe *The Greene Devils*, Mike Green und seinen Gitarristen Ouzo, die gerade für ihre neue CD den Grammy bekommen haben. Im Anschluss daran sollst du für eine Jugendzeitschrift einen Bericht über das Interview schreiben.

Setze den folgenden Dialog in die indirekte Rede und schreibe ihn in dein Heft. Beginne so:
After their fantastic new CD and the Grammy award I had the chance to interview Mike Greene and Ouzo of the Green Devils for Rock International. First of all, I congratulated Mike …

You: Hello, Mike. Congratulations on your fantastic new record. How do you feel?
M.G.: We are still pretty much exhausted. I can't believe we really won the award.
You: Are you going to celebrate tonight?
M.G.: Yes, of course. I think we'll have some of our crew and the managers over for a little party.
You: Your guitar work seems to have improved very much, Ouzo. What did you do to become so good?

Ouzo: Nothing, really. We've never had so much time to produce our album. Our manager has cancelled nearly all the gigs up to now and so the band was able to concentrate on every little detail. But please excuse me for a minute, I have to go to the bathroom.
You: Mike, he seems to be a bit nervous. Are the rumours true that he has started taking hard drugs again, since his girlfriend Amy left him?
M.G.: Don't ask about drugs, please. Our band is clean.
You: But you must admit that drugs are a great problem for a lot of musicians.
M.G.: Stop it. I'm fed up with these questions.
You: What are your plans for the rest of the season?
M.G.: We're going to play a few concerts in America and Japan. Not a big tour, and then we'll have our well-deserved holiday before we prepare our world tour in October.
You: Could you please sign this T-shirt for us? Our magazine is collecting autographs from all the stars we can get hold of. We are planning to offer the T-shirt at a charity auction which will be held next September, and we hope to get a good price for it since it is a good cause.
M.G.: What kind of cause is it for?
You: We want to build a school in Afghanistan.
M.G.: Of course, I'll support this idea.
You: Thank you for the interview.

**2** **Dies ist ein Gespräch, welches Lisa und Luke mithörten, als sie im Theater waren. Sie berichten einem Freund am nächsten Tag über dieses Gespräch. Schreibe das Originalgespräch in dein Heft.** ___/16

"You cannot imagine this strange conversation we overheard at the theatre last night. There was this man who kept complaining all the time. First he said he couldn't see properly as the man in front of him was so tall. Then he mentioned that his back was aching since his seat was not comfortable enough. He kept on asking the woman next to him when the break was because he was thirsty. Then my wife whispered to me that he must have fallen asleep because he had been quiet for some time. This was correct as his wife nudged *(mit dem Ellenbogen stoßen)* him repeatedly and told him to stop snoring. He only said he had never seen such a lousy play. A few minutes later the man wondered why the people behind them were constantly shushing *(Pst!-machen)*. The man's wife finally asked him to be quiet. She suggested that he should either close his eyes and go to sleep or just sit and watch. Insulted by these remarks, he got up and left and everybody – including me – was really pleased about this."

**Gesamtpunktzahl** ___/46

# 11 Comment and Composition

**Zu den wichtigsten Aufgabenformen in englischen Prüfungsarbeiten zählt der *comment*. Darunter versteht man eine Stellungnahme zu einem gestellten Thema, welches meist aktuellen Bezug hat. Im Folgenden werden wesentliche Vorgehensweisen bei der Erstellung eines kommentierenden Textes erläutert und Grundlagen der freien Texterstellung *(composition)* aufgezeigt.**

## 11.1 Richtig gliedern

Regel

**Die Grundgliederung im *Comment***

Ein kommentierender Text zeigt meistens folgende Gliederung:

<table>
<tr><td colspan="2">1. Einleitung (introduction)<br>Hinführung zum Thema, etwa durch die Herstellung eines aktuellen Bezugs, durch die Verwendung einer rhetorischen Frage, etc.</td></tr>
<tr><td colspan="2">2. Hauptteil (main body)<br>Behandlung des eigentlichen Themas, meist in dialektischer Form (Pro und Kontra) blockweise (zuerst Vorteile, dann Nachteile) oder gekreuzt</td></tr>
<tr><td>2.1 Argumente/Beispiele Pro<br>in aufzählender Weise<br>(enumeration)</td><td>2.2 Argumente/Beispiele Kontra<br>in aufzählender Weise<br>(enumeration)</td></tr>
<tr><td colspan="2">3. Schlussfolgerung (conclusion)<br>evtl. mit kurzer Zusammenfassung und abschließender Bemerkung</td></tr>
</table>

Für jedes dieser in der Tabelle dargestellten Segmente benötigt man eine Art **Werkzeugkasten**, d.h. eine Sammlung an sprachlichen Mitteln, mit denen man einleiten, hinführen, kontrastieren, aufzählen und schlussfolgern kann. Somit wird die Aufgabenform des *comment* eigentlich recht gut kalkulierbar.

**1** Erstelle aus den Notizen eine tabellarische Grundgliederung für einen *comment* auf Englisch.

**Thema:** The Internet – paradise or hell? Discuss.

**Intro:** neuere Untersuchungen: Kinder verbringen viel zu lange Zeit vor dem PC; seit Jahren: hitzige Diskussionen zu diesem Thema;

**Hinführung:** Bringt das Internet eher Nutzen oder schadet es?

**Hauptteil**

Argumente pro Internet:
schneller Zugriff auf Informationen, Möglichkeit der Kontaktaufnahme (*chats*, *skype*, etc.), Internet als Warenhaus, Internet als Spielbereich *(gaming)*;

Argumente kontra Internet:
Gefahr der Abhängigkeit, vermeintlicher Kontakt bei doch fehlender persönlicher Begegnung, Preisgabe von persönlichen Daten, etc.

Schlussfolgerung: zusammenfassende Bemerkung, abschließende Beurteilung;

**Intro**

**main body**

| **pros** | **cons** |
| --- | --- |
| | |

**conclusion**

Tipp

**Plural bedeutet mindestens drei!**

In einem *comment* solltest du für jede Argumentationsrichtung mehrere Argumente oder Beispiele anfügen. Mehrere bedeutet Plural und der Plural besteht hier ausnahmsweise aus mindestens drei! Andernfalls wird die Argumentationskette in deinem Text einfach zu dünn.

Tipp

### Die eigene Meinung

Halte dich grundsätzlich mit deiner eigenen Meinung in der Einleitung und im Hauptteil deutlich zurück. Erst in der abschließenden Bemerkung und der Schlussfolgerung solltest du persönlich Stellung nehmen – wenn die Themenstellung dies fordert. Man kann ganz wunderbar gute, kommentierende Text schreiben, in denen kein einziges Mal ein ich *(I)* vorkommt.

Vermeide auf jeden Fall vereinfachte Wendungen wie *I think …* oder *I (must) say that … .*

## 11.2 Richtig einleiten

Regel

### Die Einleitung *(introduction)*

Für die Einleitung benötigst du zwei Dinge: eine **gute Idee**, um auf das Thema hinzuführen, und **sprachliche Mittel** in Form bestimmter Wendungen:

| Ideen | Sprachliche Mittel, z. B. |
|---|---|
| Bezug zu einem aktuellen Ereignis/einer aktuellen Entwicklung | *Last week's incidents in New York have illustrated well that …* |
| Aufgreifen eines bekannten Zitats oder eines Sprichworts | *'No sports', Churchill once responded when asked if …* |
| Aufwerfen einer provokativen Frage/einer provokativen Aussage | *Smoking makes you slim and slender. This is what can often be seen on posters picturing …* |
| Schilderung eines (scheinbaren) Kontrasts | *Beauty is a mess for some, and a bliss for others.* |
| Schilderung einer persönlichen Erfahrung | *It was not more than a month ago when I …* |
| Standard-Einleitungsphrase (die schlechteste Idee) | *There has been a heated controversy over the question if …; It has often been said/claimed/assumed that …;* |

**2** Schreibe in deinem Heft je einen Einleitungssatz zu den folgenden Themen.

a) wisdom
b) school uniform
c) addiction
d) tradition

## 11.3 Richtig aufzählen, graduieren, einschränken, abwägen und schlussfolgern

Regel

**Beispiele für sprachliche Mittel bei Aufzählungen**

- **allgemeine:** *Various reasons may account for … - We must bear several points in mind when discussing about … - There are many different reasons for people getting …*
- **chronologisch:** *Firstly, … - Secondly, … - Thirdly, … - In the first place … - In the second place … - For one thing … - … for another … - First of all, … - To begin with … - Let us start by saying that … - Then … - Besides, … - Moreover, … - Furthermore, … - In addition to this … - Additionally, … - Last of all, … - Finally, …*

**Beispiele für sprachliche Mittel bei Graduierungen**

*It is important to state that … - It deserves mentioning that … - Similarly striking is the fact that … - A more important aspect can be seen in the fact that … - Better/Worse still is the fact that … - What is most important of all is …*

**Beispiele für sprachliche Mittel bei Einschränkungen**

*… yet/still … - Nevertheless … - In spite of this … - Even so … - Despite … - Although/Though … - … but actually … - Contrary to …*

**Beispiele für sprachliche Mittel bei Abwägungen**

*… but otherwise … - On the one hand …, on the other hand … - … on the contrary … - … however … - A comparison of A and B will prove that …*

**Beispiele für sprachliche Mittel bei Schlussfolgerungen**

*Therefore … - For these reasons … - Consequently, … - Thus … - This finally implies that … - To conclude … - In conclusion … - Taking all the arguments mentioned into consideration/account … - Summing up … - In short …*

**3** Übersetze.

a) Aus den erwähnten Gründen kann man sagen, dass … ______________________

______________________________________________

b) Trotz dieser Entwicklung … ______________________________

______________________________________________

c) Über dieses Thema wurde schon sehr häufig diskutiert. ______________________

______________________________________________

66 Aus welchen Teilen besteht ein *comment* grundsätzlich?

67 Wie viele Argumente sollte man in einem *comment* mindestens anführen?

68 Wie nennt man auf Englisch die Argumente, die für etwas, wie die, die gegen etwas sprechen?

69 Führe die Aufzählungen fort.

a) Firstly, …

b) On the one hand, …

c) To begin with …

70 Nenne drei Möglichkeiten, Einschränkungen auszudrücken.

a)

b)

c)

71 Wo in einem *comment* sollte man persönlich Stellung zum Thema beziehen?

72 Formuliere einen Einleitungssatz zum Thema *Werbung in der Schule.*

73 Wie übersetzt man *Aus all diesen Gründen …*?

74 Wie übersetzt man *Einerseits …, andererseits …*?

1 Wähle eines der folgenden Themen und schreibe einen kommentierenden Text. ___/30

a) Should PC games presenting too much violence be prohibited? Discuss.
b) "You are what you eat." Discuss.
c) Is Europe at its end? Discuss.

Gesamtpunktzahl ___/30

# 12 *Cartoons:* Karikaturen

**Eine Karikatur *(cartoon)* stellt Menschen, eine bestimmte Situation oder ein Problem auf komische und überzeichnete Weise dar. Durch Übertreibung und Verzerrung werden so z.B. politische Verhältnisse ins Bewusstsein des Betrachters gerückt, der dann zum Nachdenken angeregt wird.**

## 12.1 Dargestellte Situation

Regel

**Beschreibung der dargestellten Situation**

Es gibt unterschiedliche Meinungen darüber, wie man an die Interpretation einer Karikatur herangehen sollte. Die einen schlagen zunächst eine Beschreibung dessen, was man an Details sieht, vor, die anderen wollen zuerst die Botschaft, die eine Karikatur enthält, aufarbeiten.
Wir schlagen zunächst eine **Beschreibung der Situation**, **nicht der Details** vor.

**1** Beschreibe die in der Karikatur dargestellte Situation (nicht die einzelnen Details!) in zwei bis drei englischen Sätzen. Schreibe in dein Heft.

## 12.2 Botschaft und Interpretation

**2** Formuliere für die Karikatur in Aufgabe 1 die Botschaft/Kritik in ein bis zwei englischen Sätzen.

Regel

**Die Interpretation**

**Belege** nun die in Aufgabe 2 präsentierte **Botschaft mit Details**. Verwende hierbei aber nur die Details, die für die Interpretation der Botschaft wichtig sind. Verwende das *present progressive* um das, was in der Karikatur getan wird, zu beschreiben.

Tipp

**Botschaften in Karikaturen beschreiben**

Die folgenden Wendungen können bei der **Beschreibung der Botschaft** hilfreich sein:

+ Ich denke, die Karikatur soll X kritisieren → *According to my opinion, the cartoon is supposed to criticize X.*
+ … soll die Unwissenheit und das Fehlverhalten des Menschen verbalisieren → *… is to verbalize human ignorance and behaviour*
+ verurteilen/lächerlich machen/verspotten/lustig machen über → *condemn/ridicule/mock/poke fun at/make fun of*
+ Der Karikaturist könnte die Botschaft vermitteln wollen, dass … → *The cartoonist might want to convey/present the message that …*
+ auf etwas anspielen → *to allude to;* eine Anspielung auf → *an allusion to*
+ eine leichte/starke Übertreibung → *a slight/gross exaggeration*
+ … bezieht sich auf das Problem der politischen Instabilität → *… refers to the problem of political instability*
+ … stellt ein verzerrtes Bild von X dar → *… reflects a distorted image of/about X*
+ … im übertragenen Sinn … → *… on the figurative level …/… figuratively …*
+ Seine Absicht könnte sein, … → *His intention might be to …*
+ Man könnte den Schluss ziehen, dass … → *You might draw the conclusion that …*

Tipp

**Begriffe und Wendungen für die Interpretation**

Die folgenden Begriffe und Wendungen können bei der Interpretation der Botschaft hilfreich sein:
Analyse → *analysis*; Bildunterschrift → *caption*; Sprechblase → *speech bubble*; Gedankenblase → *thought bubble*; versteckter Hinweis auf → *hidden hint/reference to*; Gesichtsausdruck → *facial expression*; Körperhaltung → *posture*; Geste → *gesture*; Mimik → *facial expression*; Charaktereigenschaft → *trait*

3 Schreibe in deinem Heft eine Interpretation der Karikatur der Aufgabe 1.

## Training plus

75 Bringe die folgenden Begriffe in die richtige chronologische Reihenfolge:
Interpretation • Beschreibung der Situation • Darstellung der Botschaft

______________________________

76 Denjenigen (oder diejenige), der (oder die) eine Karikatur angefertigt hat, nennt man ______________________ .

77 Sprechblase und Denkblase heißen im Englischen ______________________ und ______________________.

78 Bildunterschrift nennt man im Englischen ______________________.

79 Gesichtsausdruck, Körperhaltung und Mimik heißen im Englischen

______________________________.

80 Übersetze den folgenden Satz ins Englische.
Der Karikaturist bezieht sich auf das Problem der Massenarbeitslosigkeit.

______________________________

______________________________

1 Interpretiere die Karikatur „How to get rid of smokers." ___/20

Gesamtpunktzahl ___/20

# 13 Texte zusammenfassen und Mediation

**Eine Zusammenfassung *(summary)* eines Sachtextes ist keine leichte Aufgabe. Welche Informationen sind wesentlich und deshalb unverzichtbar? Welche schmücken den Text nur aus?**

## 13.1 Fasse dich kürzer! (I)

Regel

***Summary***

Ein ***summary*** fasst die wichtigsten inhaltlichen Aspekte *(Who? What? When? Where? Why? How?)*, die Grundgedanken und die Hauptargumente eines Textes zusammen.

- Zusammenfassungen werden, wie im Deutschen, grundsätzlich im ***present tense*** verfasst.
- **Namen** und **Details**, die **für die Sinnerfassung unwichtig** sind, also z.B. **Zahlen, Beispiele, Zitate, Illustrationen, Sprichwörter, Ironie, Symbole** und **alle Mittel**, die ein Autor verwendet, um einen Text lebhafter oder witziger zu gestalten, gehen nicht in das ***summary*** ein.
- Ist es nötig, direkte Rede zu verwenden, muss diese in die indirekte Rede ***(reported speech)*** übertragen werden.
- **Äußerungen der eigenen Meinung oder persönliche Kritik sind nicht erlaubt.**
- Bei der Erstellung des zusammengefassten Textes sollten **eigene Formulierungen** verwendet werden.
- Der **Textaufbau** des Originalautors kann, aber **muss nicht verwendet werden**.

**1** Entscheide welche Informationen für eine Zusammenfassung wichtig sind.

**Hulking Cargo Ships Off Singapore**

When Sun Lee, a 24-year-old secretary from Bedok, Singapore, looks out of her window she sees an uncommon sight: hundreds of cargo ships lying idle, like an endless herd of sleeping elephants just outside Singapore's port. So many ships have gathered here that some companies are worried about accidents in one of the world's most congested waterways, the Strait of Malacca, which separates Singapore and Malaysia from Indonesia.

"Some of the ships weigh up to 270 000 metric tons," says Harvey Johnson, executive at a Singapore broker firm, "That's more that the entire Spanish Armada weighed!" They are floating on the water, rather than in it. Their red rudders and round noses, submerged when loaded, are sticking several meters high out of the water.

The root of the problem lies in the great decrease in international trade. China's exports have slumped more than 22 % since last year, the exports of the Philippines more than 30%.

The West has lost interest in consumption. For an increase in trade an increase in demand is necessary. "Since consumers in the US and Europe still have to cope with their losses on the stock market, they are in no mood to start spending again!" says Johnson. "No consumption, no transport!"

Thus the cost of transporting a standard 12-meter steel container from China to Northern Europe has dropped from $1500 plus fuel charge in April 2008 to $150 plus fuel charge in 2009, which is far below the costs of providing the service.

Already eight smaller companies in the cargo business have gone bankrupt since last year, and at least one of the bigger ones is expected to follow this year.

There are a lot of ships anchored at other ports around the world, too, but nowhere are there so many as in Singapore. The ships have come here because Singapore has few storms, excellent ship repair teams and cheap fuel from its own refinery.

Most important, however, is probably its proximity to other Asian ports that might eventually have cargo.

This may still be a long time off, so Sun Lee may be able to enjoy her exotic view for quite some time.

| | wichtig | unwichtig |
|---|---|---|
| a) Sun Lee is a secretary. | ☐ | ☐ |
| b) Ships look like elephants. | ☐ | ☐ |
| c) The ships do not move. | ☐ | ☐ |
| d) The Strait of Malacca is an important waterway. | ☐ | ☐ |
| e) Some single ships are heavier than the Spanish Armada in the $16^{th}$ century. | ☐ | ☐ |
| f) The rudders stick out of the water. | ☐ | ☐ |
| g) The ships have no cargo. | ☐ | ☐ |
| h) International trade has decreased. | ☐ | ☐ |
| i) Europeans are no longer interested in buying.. | ☐ | ☐ |
| j) They have lost money on the stock markets. | ☐ | ☐ |
| k) It costs $150 to transport a container to Europe. | ☐ | ☐ |
| l) Singapore has a refinery. | ☐ | ☐ |
| m) It is close to Asian ports. | ☐ | ☐ |
| n) The situation will not change soon. | ☐ | ☐ |

## 13.2 Fasse dich kürzer! (II)

Regel

**Möglichkeiten Aussagen zu verkürzen**

- Finde **übergeordnete Begriffe.**
  **Original:** *Bond was looking under the chairs, the table, the sofa, the sideboard and even the bed, but he didn't find any microphones that could have transmitted his conversation with Felix.*
  **Zusammenfassung:** *Bond searches the furniture but doesn't find any electronic spying devices.*
- Verkürze lange Nebensätze mit ***gerunds*** und ***participles.***
  **Original:** *After he had opened the door to his bathroom he heard the car, which came slowly closer.*
  **Zusammenfassung:** *After opening the door to his bathroom he heard the car coming slowly closer.*
- Verkürze Sätze mit Infinitiven.
  **Original:** *The man who he should meet was called Scaramanga.*
  **Zusammenfassung:** *The man to meet was Scaramanga.*

**2** Finde übergeordnete Begriffe.

a) chair, table, sofa, bed, desk ____________________

b) Hinduism, Buddhism, Christianity ____________________

c) Paris Hilton, Brad Pitt, Mick Jagger ____________________

d) Reagan, Bush, Clinton, Obama ____________________

e) teacher, mechanic, engineer, cook ____________________

**3** Verkürze bzw. verbinde die folgenden Sätze mithilfe von Gerund-Konstruktionen und Partizipien.

a) Metallica's German Tour started in Munich last night. The band was working solidly through their repertoire.

b) Because they are probably the most democratic band, they were playing on a 360° stage, which was positioned in the centre of the arena.

c) Metallica has been everybody's darling after they published *Death Magnetic* in 2008.

d) Many people were waiting outside since the stadium was actually too small.

# 13.3 Fasse dich kürzer! (III)

Regel

**Schrittweises Vorgehen beim Zusammenfassen**

- **Step 1:** Lies den Text **mindestens zweimal**. Nimm dir Zeit! Finde zuerst heraus, **worum es** in dem Text grundsätzlich **geht**.
- **Step 2:** Lies den Text noch einmal und **klammere** Folgendes **ein**: wörtliche Rede - Namen und Details von Menschen, die für den Sinn unwichtig sind - Zahlen - Beispiele - Illustrationen - lustige Einschübe - Sprichwörter - Ironie - Symbole u.s.w., also alle Mittel, die ein Autor verwendet um einen Text lebhafter oder witziger zu gestalten.
- **Step 3:** Schreibe alles, was nun **nicht in Klammern** steht, notizartig auf ein extra Blatt, denn dies müssten dann die Hauptgedanken des Originaltextes sein. Dieses Blatt ist dein Konzeptpapier.
- **Step 4:** Jetzt muss das Konzept mit deinen Notizen noch in die richtige Form gebracht, also in einen sprachlich richtigen und zusammenhängenden Text verwandelt werden.
- **Step 5:** Am Ende überprüft man den Text nochmals auf Fehler. Achte auf: *present tense*, Zeitenfolge, Rechtschreibfehler, indirekte Rede.
- **Step 6:** In den meisten Fällen soll der Text eine bestimmte Anzahl an Wörtern nicht überschreiten, daher muss man am Ende noch einmal überschlägig die Wörter zählen und nötigenfalls verkürzen oder verlängern.

## 4 Textarbeit

a) Setze die unwichtige Information in Klammern.

b) Schreibe eine Textzusammenfassung in dein Heft. Wende dabei die *6 Steps* an.

**The Whistling Ape**

"I was Kaiser Bill's batman", was Whistling Jack Smith's hit in the 60s, the Scorpions whistled "Winds of Change" in the 90s, and now Ujian, an Orang Utan of the Heidelberg Zoo is pursing his lips: the zoo is releasing a CD with the whistles of the 10-year-old male.

Although he doesn't hit every note correctly he whistles the leading melody, and Tobias Kämmerer sings the pop-rock production "Ich bin Ujian" (I'm Ujian), which will be released in June.

The happy-go-lucky song, which is accompanied by heavy drumming and jungle-sounds, will be sold for € 3.99 at the zoo. All in all, five different mixes for the CD were produced including a radio version as well as a fast house-mix and even a karaoke version.

## 13.4 Mediation

Regel

***Mediation*** bedeutet, eine Vorlage aus der Originalsprache in die jeweils andere **sinngemäß** zu übertragen. Das Endprodukt der Mediation muss natürlich trotzdem sprachlich fehlerfrei sein. Beim sinngemäßen Übersetzen muss **nicht jedes Wort** verstanden oder **übersetzt** werden. Meist genügt es, wenn man die **wichtigsten Ideen** zusammenfasst und mit eigenen Worten widergibt. Kennt man ein Wort nicht, oder fällt einem ein Wort nicht ein, so kann man es **paraphrasieren**, also umschreiben.

Für beide Formen des Übertragens in eine andere Sprache muss man sich einige Fragen zum Originaltext stellen, um die Übertragung der Aufgabe richtig anpassen zu können:

- Um welchen **Texttyp** *(text type)* handelt es sich? → *narration, argumentation, exposition, description?*
- Wer ist der **Autor** und was will er? → *the author's intention?*
- Welche **Zielgruppe** hat der Text? → *audience, target group?*
- Was ist das **Ziel der Übertragung**? → *translation, interpreting for a friend, parents or business partners, summarizing in the target language?*

**Techniken der Mediation**

Durch extensives Lesen ***(skimming and scanning)*** kann man sich einen ersten Überblick verschaffen. Ziel des ***skimming*** ist es, die **Hauptgedanken** eines Textes herauszufinden (z.B. über zentrale Begriffe, ***keywords***, etc.), Ziel des ***scanning*** ist es, durch schnelles Lesen **wichtige Teilaspekte** herauszufinden. In geschriebenen Texten ist es oft sinnvoll, die einzelnen **Absätze** mit **Überschriften** zu versehen. Hat man viel Zeit, kann man auch die Techniken für das Schreiben von ***summaries*** anwenden.
**Bei unbekannten Wörtern** sollte man versuchen, **Bedeutungen abzuleiten.**
Schwierige Grammatik sollte man im Auge behalten (z.B. Gerundialkonstruktionen und Partizipien, Infinitive, indirekte Rede u.s.w.).

Tipp

Am Ende der Arbeit muss man noch einmal den Text überarbeiten. Deshalb ist es sinnvoll, immer eine Zeile zwischen dem Geschriebenen frei zu lassen, damit man hernach noch Korrekturen einarbeiten kann.

**81** In welcher Zeitform *(tense)* schreibt man im Deutschen wie im Englischen Zusammenfassungen? ____________________

**82** Wörtliche Rede muss in Textzusammenfassungen grundsätzlich in ____________________ umgewandelt werden.

**83** Fasse die Aussage in einem Satz zusammen.
*"The cost of transporting has dropped from $ 1500 in 2008, to $150 in 2009. The price for chartering a ship has gone down from $ 300 000 per day to $ 10 000."*

____________________

____________________

**84** *Skimming a text* bedeutet ____________________

**85** *Scanning a text* heißt ____________________

**86** Was ist bei einer *mediation* wichtig? ____________________

____________________

**87** *Narration, exposition, description* und *argumentation* beziehen sich auf

____________________

____________________

**88** Nenne drei Beispiele, wie man Aussagen verkürzen kann.

____________________

____________________

**89** Setze ins Englische um: Du möchtest dich zum Thema Treibhauseffekt äußern.

____________________

____________________

**90** Setze ins Englische um: Du willst deine Verärgerung über einen gestern erschienenen Zeitungsartikel zum Ausdruck bringen. ____________________

____________________

**With the click of a key, bullies are humiliating their peers. What are schools doing to tame this behavior?**

*By Amanda Paulson, Staff writer of The Christian Science Monitor*

For one middle-school girl it was a rumor, circulated via text messaging, that she had contracted SARS while on a trip to Toronto. She returned to school and found nobody would come near her. For an overweight boy in Japan, it was cellphone pictures, taken of him on the sly while he was changing in the locker room and then sent to many of his peers.

And for Calabasas High School in California, it was a website - schoolscandals.com - on which vicious gossip and racist and threatening remarks grew so rampant that most of the school was affected.

The actions themselves - rumors, threats, gossip, humiliation - are nothing new. But among today's adolescents - a generation of instant messengers, always connected, always wired - bullies are starting to move beyond slam books and whisper campaigns to e-mail, websites, chat rooms, and text messaging.

While in some ways it's no worse than old-fashioned bullying, cyberbullying has a few idiosyncrasies. Websites and screen names give bullies a mask of anonymity if they wish it, making them difficult to trace.

The pressure for kids to be always online means bullies can extend their harassment into their victims' homes.

And the miracle of the Web means that sharing an embarrassing photo or private note - with thousands of people - requires little more than the click of a key.

"It used to be if something happened at school, someone made a joke about you, or said something in front of you, that was horrible enough," says Glenn Stutzky, instructor in Michigan State University's School of Social Work.

"But at least a relatively small group of people was there and aware of it. With wireless technology, that stuff is much more quickly spread, not only around school but it has the potential of being put up and shared around the world."

No one knows that better than Ghyslain, the Canadian teenager who gained notoriety this year as "the Star Wars kid." Fooling around alone with a video camera one day, the somewhat awkward adolescent filmed himself acting out a scene from "Star Wars": He twirled and flung himself about the room, swinging a golf-ball retriever as his light saber. It was the sort of private geeky moment many kids have, but in Ghyslain's case, it went further. Some peers got hold of the video, uploaded it to the Internet, and started passing it around, splicing him into "The Matrix," "The Terminator," or the musical "Chicago," with added special effects and sounds, soon followed. He's now the most downloaded male of the year. According to news reports, he was forced to drop out of school and seek psychiatric help.

"It's one of the saddest examples," says Mr. Stutzky. "He did one goofy little thing, and now it will always be a part of that young man's life."

**Three burgers a day...**

*By Lawrence Donegan, The Observer, Sunday, June 6, 2004*

Morgan Spurlock, whose eclectic career has included stints as a corporate spokesman for Sony Electronics, an award-winning playwright and a beach volleyball commentator for America's leading cable sports TV station, was watching the news at his parents' home in West Virginia when an item came on about two teenagers from the Bronx who were suing McDonald's for making them obese. "I was stuffed with Thanksgiving turkey, watching this story, when it hit me," he recalls.

What hit Spurlock was this; for a whole month he would eat nothing but McDonald's food. Breakfast, lunch and dinner. There were three other ground rules: He had to eat every item on the McDonald's menu at least once; he could only eat what was available over the counter (no special orders); and he had to "super size" his meal whenever a counter assistant offered him the option. He would record the state of his health prior to his new diet and afterwards. If nothing else, the exercise might shed light on the teenagers' claims that fast food can seriously damage your health.

"I immediately called my friend, my director of photography Scott Ambrozy, and told him the idea." He laughed and said, "That's a really great bad idea." ....

The outcome was Super Size Me, a 98-minute documentary that follows Spurlock from pre-McDonald's health, cheer and good sex life to a post-McDonald's pit of dire health, spiritual listlessness and borderline impotency.

He was tested beforehand by three doctors and deemed to be an above average human specimen. In the first week he put on 10lbs. After the month he'd added a total of 25lbs. His cholesterol level rose by 65 points (one-third higher than when he started). Most shocking of all, his doctor, who begged the film-maker to abandon the experiment after three weeks, concluded that the constant intake of fast food was causing serious liver damage, akin to that of Nicolas Cage's character in Leaving Las Vegas. In the film's postscript, Spurlock notes that it took him 14 months to return to his former physical condition.

Spurlock's film is much more than a medical journal. Spurlock is an engaging screen presence, with a nice line in self-deprecation and perfect comic timing. In one scene he is filmed eating his first "super sized" meal in the front of his car. It begins with him gleefully rubbing his hands at the gargantuan size of the portions ... and ends with him vomiting out of the car window. ...

**1** Unterteile den Text von Seite 108 in Sinnabschnitte und schreibe neben jeden Abschnitt eine englische Überschrift. ___/5

**2** Fasse den Artikel von Seite 108 auf Deutsch für einen Freund zusammen. ___/20

**3** Schreibe eine deutsche Zusammenfassung des obenstehenden Textes für eine Schülerzeitung. ___/20

**4** Übersetze den obenstehenden Text von Zeile 19 – 31. ___/20

**Gesamtpunktzahl** ___/65

# 14 Sich zu Filmen äußern

**Filme bestehen aus behutsam zusammengestellten Szenen und Sequenzen, in denen auf kunstvolle Weise Schauspielerei, Geräusche, Musik, Spezialeffekte und vieles andere mehr kombiniert werden. Filme bieten, wie auch literarische Werke, schier unbegrenzte Möglichkeiten der Beschreibung und Interpretation.**

## 14.1 Kamera und Objekt

Regel

**Kameraeinstellungen *(camera range)***

Unter ***camera range*** versteht man die **Entfernung** zwischen aufnehmender Kamera und aufgenommenem Objekt. Man unterscheidet folgende **Einstellungen**:

- ***long shot*** (auch: ***total***): Diese ermöglicht die Darstellung des gesamten Filmsets *(set)* in einer Art Totalaufnahme.
- ***medium long shot***: Diese Einstellung zeigt eine agierende Person in ihrer filmischen Umgebung (z. B. in einer Straße).
- ***full shot***: Sie zeigt den Körper eines Darstellers im Großformat.
- ***medium shot***: Diese Einstellung zeigt den größten Teil einer Person/eines Gegenstandes, aber eben nicht die gesamte Person/den gesamten Gegenstand.
- ***close-up***: Hier wird nur noch ein Detail gezeigt, so etwa in einem Wild-West-Film die beiden unruhig flackernden Augen einer Person während eines Duells.

**1** Benenne die verwendete *camera range.*

a) ____________ b) ____________ c) ____________

**2** Übersetze ins Deutsche.

a) This fascinating scene presents a pair of eyes in a duel in close-up-camera range.

____________________________________________

____________________________________________

b) You might be able to recognize two people in life jackets in full shot camera range.

c) This total camera range gives the spectator the chance to view a wonderful scenery of lakes.

## 14.2 Richtung und Bewegung

Regel

**Kameraperspektive *(camera angle)* und Kamerabewegung *(camera movement)***

Die **Kameraperspektive** beschreibt die **Richtung**, aus der ein Objekt betrachtet wird: Der ***aerial shot*** zeigt eine Betrachtung des aufgenommenen Objekts von schräg oben. Dadurch erscheint das Dargestellte kleiner und weniger wichtig. Ein ***eye-level shot*** zeigt etwas auf Augenhöhe. Da dies eine natürliche Perspektive ist, wird der *eye-level shot* immer dann verwendet, wenn etwas möglichst objektiv dargestellt werden soll. Der ***low-angle shot*** zeigt das Dargestellte von schräg unten. Hierdurch entsteht ein finsterer, teilweise bedrohlicher Eindruck.

Während eines ***panning shot*** bewegt sich die Kamera horizontal von links nach rechts (oder umgekehrt). Die vertikale Kamerabewegung nennt man ***tilt shot***. Bei einem ***tracking shot*** verfolgt man mit der Kamera ein sich bewegendes Objekt. Ein **zoom** schließlich ist das Heranziehen *(zooming in)* oder Wegdrücken *(zooming out)* eines Objekts mithilfe der verstellbaren Linsen im Kameraobjektiv.

**3** Übersetze.

Charlie Chaplin wird in dieser Szene von oben aufgenommen. Eine solche Kameraperspektive nennt man *aerial shot*. Dadurch erscheint er noch lächerlicher. Später im Film wird er von der Kamera in einem *tracking shot* verfolgt, in seinem Auto fahrend gefilmt.

Info plus

### Charlie Chaplin

Sir Charles Chaplin (Sir, weil er vom britischen Königshaus geadelt wurde), genannt Charlie Chaplin (1889 bis 1977), war englischer Schauspieler, Komiker, Produzent und Regisseur. Er gilt als einer der besten und bekanntesten Komiker des 20. Jahrhunderts. Berühmt wurde er durch Filme wie *The Tramp*, *The Gold Rush*, *City Lights*, *Modern Times*, *The Great Dictator* und *Limelight*.
Chaplin trat in seinen Filmen meist als eine tragikomische Figur mit Zweifingerbart *(Chaplin Beard)*, schlotternder Hose und übergroßen Schuhen, mit Bambusstock in der Hand und einer Melone auf dem Kopf sowie in enger Jacke auf.
Der Meister der Stummfilm-Komik startete seine Karriere im Kindesalter in *music halls*. Sein erster Tonfilm, *The Great Dictator*, wurde erstmalig 1940 gezeigt. In ihm spielte er in satirischer Weise einen verspielten Diktator, der die Welt beherrschen möchte – eine Anspielung auf Adolf Hitler und dessen nationalsozialistische Schreckensherrschaft. Charlie Chaplin hat in fast 100 Filmen mitgewirkt und dafür 26 Auszeichnungen renommierter Institutionen erhalten.

Tipp

### Filme/Szenen kritisch betrachten und hinterfragen

Beim kritischen Betrachten von Filmen geht man wie bei der Arbeit mit Texten vor. Man unterteilt den Film in **Abschnitte** (Szenenblöcke, Szenen) und sieht sich diese vor dem Hintergrund einer bestimmten Fragestellung (z. B. Inhalt, Filmtechniken, Musik, Geräusche) an. Die Ergebnisse dieser Betrachtung können in einer Art **Filmlogbuch** *(viewing log)* festgehalten werden. Dabei sind folgende Fragestellungen wichtig: Was sieht man? Wie sieht man die Szene? Welche Einstellung, welche Perspektive, welche Kamerabewegung ist erkennbar? Welche **Funktionen** haben diese kameratechnischen Vorgehensweisen? In welcher Weise tragen Hintergrundmusik, Geräusche und Schnitt *(cut)* zum filmischen Ausdruck bei?

Info plus

## Filmischer Wortschatz und filmische Wendungen

**Filmischer Wortschatz**

| | |
|---|---|
| *shot/scene* | Szene |
| *camera perspective/angle* | Kameraperspektive |
| *camera range* | Kameraentfernung zum Objekt |
| *camera movement* | Kamerabewegung |
| *cut* | Schnitt |
| *shot sequence* | Filmsequenz/Schnittfolge |
| *fading in/out* | Ein-/Ausblenden |
| *back lighting* | Gegenlicht |
| *cross cutting* | Hin- und Herspringen zwischen zwei Aufnahmelokalitäten |
| *flashback* | zeitlicher Rückblick auf eine Szene in der Vergangenheit |
| *flash forward/forshadowing* | zeitlicher Ausblick auf eine Szene in der Zukunft |
| *parallel shot* | zwei Aktionen werden abwechselnd zeitlich parallel gezeigt |
| *slow motion* | Zeitlupe |
| *sound track* | alle Musikstücke zu einem Film |
| *swish pan* | Kamerabewegung, die so schnell ist, dass die Bilder unscharf und verzerrt erscheinen |
| *voice over* | Kommentar eines unsichtbaren Erzählers |
| *character* | Darsteller |
| *director* | Regisseur |
| *producer* | Produzent |
| *film production* | Filmproduktion |
| *storyboard* | Drehbuch |

**Filmische Wendungen**

*The camera is at a short/long/medium distance to … – The shot is presented from a low/high angle to put emphasis on …. – This close-up shows … – The opening scene captures an atmosphere of … – The character's frightened facial expressions indicates that … – The body language expresses the character's attitude towards … – The director achieves an effect of … – He makes use of flashbacks in order to … – The background music is subtle thus conveying an effect of … – The sound effects create an atmosphere of … – The action on screen takes place in/at … – The camera pans/zooms in to show that …*

**91** Kameraperspektive und Kamerabewegung werden im Englischen

______________________ und ______________________ genannt.

**92** Zooming in bedeutet, dass ______________________________________

______________________________________________________.

**93** Ein zeitlicher Rückblick in einer Szene, die in der Vergangenheit spielt, nennt

man ______________________________________________ .

**94** Ein zeitlicher Ausblick in einer Szene, die in der Zukunft spielt, nennt man

______________________________________________________.

**95** Die Person, die im Regiestuhl sitzt, nennt man ______________________.

**96** - **99** Übersetze die folgenden Begriffe.

- **96** Schnittfolge: ______________________________________
- **97** Gegenlicht: ______________________________________
- **98** Darsteller: ______________________________________
- **99** einblenden: ______________________________________

1 Suche dir eine wichtige Szene aus einem bekannten Film deiner Wahl heraus und beschreibe die filmtechnischen und inhaltlichen Komponenten un deren Funktion. ___/30

Gesamtpunktzahl ___/30

**Allgemeine Hinweise zum Abschlusstest**
Damit du deine Gesamtpunktzahl einfach errechnen kannst, gibt es für jede Teilaufgabe bei Lückenaufgaben in der Regel einen Punkt, bei Übersetzungsaufgaben oder schwierigeren Aufgaben zwei Punkte.
Leider ist es nicht möglich, einen allgemeingültigen Notenschlüssel vorzugeben. Er wechselt von Schule zu Schule, von Bundesland zu Bundesland. Damit du deine Leistung einschätzen kannst, gibt es folgende Orientierungspunkte:
- Wenn du mehr als 80 Prozent der Gesamtpunktzahl erreicht hast, ist dein Ergebnis gut oder besser.
- Wenn du mehr als 50 Prozent der Gesamtpunktzahl erreicht hast, ist dein Ergebnis ausreichend oder befriedigend.
- Wenn du weniger als 50 Prozent der Gesamtpunktzahl erreicht hast, ist dein Ergebnis nicht mehr ausreichend. Du solltest dann die Regeln und Aufgaben, bei denen du viele Fehler gemacht hast, noch einmal genau nachlesen und üben.

| 100 bis 80 Prozent | 79 bis 50 Prozent | unter 50 Prozent |
|---|---|---|
| sehr gut bis gut | befriedigend bis ausreichend | nicht mehr ausreichend |

# Kapitel 1: Zusammenschau der englischen *tenses*

## Aufgaben

**Seite 8**

1 **simple present**: He goes … They hide … It works … She talks … They flee … I walk …
Present Progressive … You are trying … She is doing … I am holding … He is running … I am leaving … ou are sleeping …
**simple past**: She jumped … We kicked … I gave … They created … He thought … You bit …
**past progressive**: He was talking … They were putting … It was raining … She was going … You were speaking … I was thinking;
**simple present perfect**: He has tried … They have hidden … I have sent … We have changed … You have lost … She has thrown …
**present perfect progressive**: She has been listening … It has been running … He has been saying … They have been teaching … We have been ringing … You have been showing …
**simple past perfect**: He had left … They had gone … She had kicked … We had beaten … It had happened … They had sold …
**past perfect progressive**: They had been watching … He had been sitting … You had been driving … We had been holding … Mary had been swimming … I had been working …
**simple future**: You will dive … We will spend … He will stay …
**future progressive**: I will be setting … You will be hiding … She will be running …

**Seite 11**

2 a) No, I'm **telling** you the truth.
b) … it **melts**.
c) It **has rained**.
d) She **has worked** …
e) **Have** you ever **been** to Scotland? - No, I **haven't**.
f) **Has** he **posted** the letter?

3 a) Michel has been sitting in the shed for two hours.
b) He doesn't know why.
c) But his father always sends him to the shed whenever he has done crazy things/misbehaved.
d) Though he always tries to be nice, he has spent five afternoons in the shed this week.
e) He's carving a wooden figure.

f) He always does this when he is in the shed.
g) This week he has made five wooden figures.
h) The last one looks like his teacher.

4 **started:** Zeitpunkt in der Vergangenheit; **had**: sich wiederholende Tätigkeit in der Vergangenheit; **were:** Zustand in der Vergangenheit; **said:** Zeitpunkt in der Vergangenheit; **need:** direkte Rede; **wasn't:** Zustand in der Vergangenheit; **was:** Zustand in der Vergangenheit; **were:** Zustand in der Vergangenheit; **was**: Zeitpunkt/Zustand in der Vergangenheit; **had cleaned:** Vorvergangenheit; **came:** Ereignis in der Vergangenheit; **said:** Ereignis in der Vergangenheit; **has got:** wörtliche Rede; **must:** wörtliche Rede/*auxiliary*; **did not like:** Zustand in der Vergangenheit; **thought:** Zustand in der Vergangenheit; **got to:** Ereignis in der Vergangenheit; **was waiting:** Handlung in der Vergangenheit, **had opened.** Vorvergangenheit, **arrived:** Ereignis in der Vergangenheit; **didn't have:** Ereignis in der Vergangenheit; **was:** Zustand in der Vergangenheit; **had been cleaning:** Handlung in der Vorvergangenheit; **came/ordered:** Ereignis in der Vergangenheit; **were laughing/having fun:** Handlung in der Vergangenheit; **left:** Ereignis in der Vergangenheit; **collected/noticed:** Ereignis in der Vergangenheit; **had not left:** Vorvergangenheit Seite 13

5 had left school; started an apprenticeship; He was talking to; a tall man came in; The man was sorting; when Alan's phone rang; Alan picked it up; put it down; a voice said; The man was filling; he dropped his pen; Alan was waiting; When he turned around; The man came; He wanted to open; and handed; Alan was sweating when he was taking;

6 Anna **will be** sixteen this summer. She **is going to have** a big party with all her friends and hopes they **will give** her great presents. Her parents **will not be** home as they **are going to fly** to Greece for their summer holidays. Her friend Clara advised her, "Don't invite Lukas and his friends. They **will drink** all night and then you **will have to clean** your house for hours." "When **are your parents leaving**?" - "Their plane **leaves** two days before my birthday." "Why **will they go** away?" - "They **are going to meet** friends in Greece." Seite 14

7 a) Next week I'm going to meet my pen-friend from Scotland. Seite 15
b) Her flight will arrive/arrives in Frankfurt on Monday.
c) She is going to spend some days with her brother in Würzburg.
d) I hope, she doesn't/won't drink too much wine, when she's here.
e) When she comes to my house she will certainly be tired.
f) As soon as I am 18, I will start driving lessons.
g) My birthday is in May, so I will have passed the test in summer.
h) Tomorrow I am going to buy a travel guide about Scotland.

## Training plus

1 *simple*: bei Handlungen/Ereignissen, die immer wieder so ablaufen; bei Aufzählungen in der Vergangenheit Seite 16
*progressive*: die Handlung oder ein andauernder Zustand wird betont
2 Es bezieht sich auf die Gegenwart (Handlung andauernd bis zur Gegenwart oder darüber hinaus).
3 *simple past tense*: Steht für abgeschlossene Handlungen/Ereignisse in der Vergangenheit.
*simple present perfect*: Steht für Handlungen/Zustände, die in der Vergangenheit begonnen haben und bis zur Gegenwart reichen.
4 *simple present perfect* und *present perfect progressive*
5 bei einer Intention oder wenn ein Plan gemacht wurde oder wenn alle Anzeichen dafür sprechen, dass etwas gleich passieren wird
6 bei offiziellen Informationen, z.B. bei Nachrichten und Fahrplänen

### Abschlusstest

**Seite 17** 1 *Simple present*: She teaches her son Latin. *Present progressive*: She's teaching her son Latin. *Simple past*: She taught her son Latin. *Simple present perfect*: She has taught her son Latin. *Present perfect progressive*: She has been teaching her son Latin. *Simple past perfect*: She had taught her son Latin. *Past perfect progressive*: She had been teaching her son Latin. *Simple will-future*: She will teach her son Latin. *Simple future perfect*: She will have taught her son Latin. *Going to-future*: She's going to teach her son Latin.

2 My wife and I **have never been** to Ireland. Last summer we **decided** to go on holiday to France, although I **have been** to France about ten times already. But my wife **hasn't agreed**. I **haven't had** a chance to go to Scotland. It's always the same!

3 a) Sir John has been awarded fourteen prizes.
b) I was watching a Steven Spielberg movie when suddenly there was a loud bang.
c) Are you going to go to school tomorrow? – No, I have been ill (sick) for four days.

| 24 – 19 Punkte | 18 – 12 Punkte | unter 12 Punkte |
|---|---|---|
| sehr gut bis gut | befriedigend bis ausreichend | nicht mehr ausreichend |

## Kapitel 2: *Passive Voice:* das Passiv

### Aufgaben

**Seite 19** 1 is being left; had been known; was being checked; was washed; was known; will be watched; have been beaten; will have been taken; was going to be fought;

**Seite 20** 2 a) The ship is being loaded by the sailors.
b) The story will have been told.
c) The problem had been talked over again and again.
d) Her exam is going to be finished by her on Monday.
e) Will the journey be booked?

3 was discovered; were stolen/had been stolen; had been smashed; was entered by; was forced open; were cut; by the burglars; were not left; was not noticed; is not secured by; are offered; will be paid by.

**Seite 21** 4 A sound in the backyard was heard by the young lady. She told her brother but she was laughed at. When she went into their garden she was passed by a man in dark clothes. She was asked, "What are you doing here?" She screamed and all of a sudden the lights were switched on by all the neighbours. She was hit on the head by the man, but he was bitten by her dog. The police was called by her father. He had been woken up by her scream. She was found in the garden. Later all the questions were answered by her.

### Training plus:

**Seite 22** 7 I'll be seventy-five (I'm going to be seventy-five) next month.

8 kein

9 … wird der Agierende betont, in einem passiven das Getane.

10 a) *present progressive* b) *past progressive*

11 Subjekt

12 Wenn es wichtig erscheint, dass der Handelnde genannt wird.

### Abschlusstest

Seite 23

1 a) The dishes are being washed by Sarah.
b) The plates have been carried into the kitchen by Michael.
c) The dining-room was being vacuum-cleaned by Susan.
d) Has the floor under the sofa been cleaned?
e) After the dustbin had been emptied, it was dropped by Michael.

2 a) During the party Michael said to Susan's girlfriend Laura: "My motorbike is checked regularly."
b) It was taken to the garage by Sarah yesterday.
c) While they were going back to the dining-room, they saw that a window was being opened.
d) Has our garden been shown to you?/Have you been shown our garden?

| 23 – 18 Punkte | 18 – 12 Punkte | unter 12 Punkte |
|---|---|---|
| sehr gut bis gut | befriedigend bis ausreichend | nicht mehr ausreichend |

## Kapitel 3: Modale Hilfsverben

### Aufgaben

Seite 25

1 a) They will have to look for Mike's bike.
b) They didn't have to look at the station.
c) Susan will be allowed/will be able to go to the shopping centre.
d) Tom, you haven't been allowed to pick your nose.
e) I hadn't been able to phone the police.
f) She had to give back the mobile.
g) Susan could not be quiet.

Seite 26

2 Mum, **can/may** I ask you a question? – Yes, you **can/may**. – I like porridge! **Can** I have porridge for breakfast in New York? – No, you **can't**. They only have coffee in New York! – **Must** I have coffee, too, or **can** I drink tea in the mornings? – No, you **needn't** have coffee. You **can** have milk in the mornings. – **Can** I have a cup of tea now? – Yes, you **can**. Maybe your sisters would like something to drink, too. Why don't you ask them? – **Could** you do that, Mum? They always hit me. – You **must** go to sleep now, Mike! It's already very late and we **must** get up very early tomorrow morning. – **Can** I finish my computer game? – No, you **can't/mustn't**. – Why **can't** I stay here a little longer? My sisters are still up. They **needn't** go to bed. – You **mustn't** yell at me, Mike! – But I'm not yelling! I **must** speak up, because otherwise you can't hear me. Susan and Tina are talking so loudly! – You **mustn't** say nasty things about your

sisters! – I **can't** say anything nice about them! – You are nasty, Mike! You **must** sleep in the attic!

**Seite 27**

3 a) Vermutung b) Frage c) Anweisung d) Übereinkunft
e) moralische Verpflichtung

4 a) Shall I open the door?
b) We are not supposed to play around with the lighter.
c) The janitor was to open the door for us.
d) Is this rope supposed to be safe?
e) You ought to have learned these words.
f) Your mother told me that you ought to be in bed by nine.

**Seite 28**

5 a) had left b) left c) Let us not
d) must have it; let him e) has left f) took their time; have
g) left h) Let us not

**Seite 29**

6 There will/is going to be great weather …; It will be sunny …; … although there may be …; Then there will be sunshine …; … the temperature may reach …; The good weather should continue …; although there might be …

## Training plus

**Seite 31**

13 Sie geben der Aussage eine Färbung.

14 be + past participle

15 Der Fuchs gibt der Ente einen Rat.

16 need not (needn't)

17 let – He let her go.

18 make s.b. do s.th. – He made her clean her room.

19 Ersatzform – may ➞ has/have been allowed to; can ➞ has have been able to

20 leave

## Abschlusstest

**Seite 32**

1 a) Shall I wash Dad's car?
b) Is this key supposed to open the suitcase?
c) He should have studied harder.
d) I should go to my room and learn for the Maths test.

2 a) Pa, Anne doesn't/won't leave me alone!
b) Can't you be serious? You mustn't make such a noise all the time.
c) Let's talk it over calmly.
d) Mike always makes me do all the housework. And he says he must learn for his test.
e) Take your time with your work.
f) I will make Mike help you with your homework. You needn't (mustn't) complain.

g) Then he left the newspaper on the table.

| 33 – 26 Punkte | 25 – 16 Punkte | unter 16 Punkte |
|---|---|---|
| sehr gut bis gut | befriedigend bis ausreichend | nicht mehr ausreichend |

## Kapitel 4: *Gerunds:* Gerund-Konstruktionen

### Aufgaben

1 going, speaking, crying, learning, getting, playing, saying, hurrying, riding, writing, reading, coming, thinking, voting, walking, swimming, trying, lying Seite 34

2 a) Skiing can be dangerous. b) Singing is fun. Seite 35
c) Reading can be interesting. d) Studying is sometimes boring.
e) Lying on the beach is my favourite hobby.

3 a) He was crazy about teasing his sister. Seite 36
b) She was sometimes angry about being teased and she was thinking about taking revenge.
c) All humans are interested in getting news.
d) Welsh people are famous for singing.
e) They are proud of having a long tradition.

4 Harry **enjoys** playing field hockey. He is a goalkeeper. He **is good at catching** balls. He **is proud of playing** in the schoolteam. He **likes** it better than **sitting** in the classroom. His sister **is crazy about** horses. She **has got** the biggest collection of books about horses at the school and she **isn't interested in** doing any sports. She **dislikes going** out and **is** only **interested** in **sitting** in her room, except when she can go to Linley's farm to watch the horses. Their mother would **enjoy having** a son who is good at school and a daughter who **is not interested in watching** TV.

5 a) After washing his face … b) Always being late … Seite 37
c) Although being hungry … d) After leaving his office …
e) … without looking around.

6 a) His boss was standing behind him saying … Seite 38
b) Apart from being late every day, you spen half an hour at the cafeteria every morning.
c) Come to my office once again before leaving the building/house.
d) Instead of eating you should work.
e) Go to your office without making a detour.

7 a) Mrs Jones is interested in her son Mike being successful. Seite 39
b) She insists on her daughter Susan repeating last year's grammar.
c) She doesn't like her children playing games all day long.
d) She can't cope with her dog sitting on the sofa.
e) She complains about her husband never helping in the kitchen.
f) Mr Jones is used to his wife having a bad day.

**Seite 41** 8 Susan had a terrible toothache. Although she had taken a pill, her bad tooth went on **hurting**. She tried **to phone** her dentist **to make** an appointment but found out that he was on holiday.
"Try **to talk** to Dr Alb." Her colleague advised her. - "I don't want **to leave** my old dentist, but I would really love **to get rid** of my tooth-ache. As usual, her tooth stopped **aching** after she had made the appointment. She had so much work that she forgot **to go**. When in the evening her toothache started again Susan regretted **forgetting** her appointment. The next morning, on her way to work she stopped **to call** at Dr Alb's, "I meant **to be** here in time yesterday but my tooth had stopped **hurting**. I hate **disappointing** people.

## Training plus

**Seite 42** 21 Subjekts, Objekts

22 a) Sie waren an hartes Arbeiten gewöhnt.
b) Sie sind daran gewöhnt, den Tisch abzuräumen.
c) Sie waren früher einmal Piloten.

23 a) being beaten
b) being unloaded
c) being respected

24 a) good at
b) tired of
c) depend on
d) interested in

25 b) ist gesünder, da mit dem Rauchen ganz aufgehört wird

26 Wunsch

## Abschlusstest

**Seite 43**

a) walking; taking
b) talking
c) hearing; being
d) her answering; to switch on
e) doing; doing
f) making; relaxing
g) me ringing; congratulating
h) to forget; worrying
i) to enjoy; sitting
j) talking; convincing; saying; telling; listening; improving
k) having to leave; shopping
l) of stealing; having taken/taking
m) driving; to let; play(ing)

| 30 – 24 Punkte | 23 – 15 Punkte | unter 15 Punkte |
|---|---|---|
| sehr gut bis gut | befriedigend bis ausreichend | nicht mehr ausreichend |

# Kapitel 5: Partizipien

1 sell - selling - having sold; write - being written - having been written; cheat - cheating - having cheated; switch on - being switched on - having been switched on; drive - driving - having driven; help - being helped - having been helped; waste - wasting - having wasted; buy - being bought - having been bought Seite 44

2 a) Falling prices are bad for business. Seite 45
b) Catweazle stayed/remained sitting calmly. Touchwood heard him breathing. The Normans came running through the forest and were searching for the old magician. They watched him climbing through the window. Then they saw him jumping into the water.
c) This was a moving view. They were standing in front of the station looking at each other. Then they stayed, hugging one another. However, she didn't notice him looking nervously at his watch. He had heard the train leaving.

3 a) The alarm-clock having rung, Mr Strange left the bedroom very quietly not wanting to wake up his wife. Seite 46
b) Reaching the end of the building Neo turned around sharply. Jumping towards Agent Smith, he tried to hit him.
c) Not wanting to leave Morpheus in the hands of Zion, he surrendered to Agent Smith.
d) Although killing Neo, Agent Smith does not succeed.
e) After being kissed by Trinity, Neo regained his powers.
f) People became slaves the machines having taken over power.

4 a) Tom moved to LA hoping to find a better job there. Seite 47
b) Hitting the curb, John fell off his bike.
c) Wanting to go home, Al closed the shoe shop early.

5 a) Having been left alone … b) Having been born on the … Seite 48
c) After having been knocked out twice …

## Training plus

27 verbs of perception; verbs of movement and rest Seite 49

28 Beispiellösung: perception: hear, feel, see
movement and rest: sit, come, arrive

29 Adverb

30 der Zeit; des Grundes

31 Er ritt in die Nacht hinein und der Mond schien hell.

32 Aktiv

33 let somebody do s.th. (Erlaubnis); make somebody do s.th. (Anweisung)

### Abschlusstest

Seite 50

1 a) Yesterday evening I wanted to see/visit my friend Stefan.
b) When sitting in the car, I asked my wife if she had locked the garden gate.
c) Having forgotten this, my wife went back quickly.
d) After having waited for ten minutes, I became impatient and went back to the house, too.
e) Standing at the door, I heard someone shouting my name.
f) Looking through the window I noticed two men talking to my wife.
g) After grabbing a spade standing next to the door, I ran in.
h) Reaching/Having reaches the living room I saw the men disappearing through the garden.
i) Policemen were going from house to house, warning people against burglars.

2 a) Being quite forgetful, I …
b) … hanging everywhere in our house …
c) After having found one sticking …
d) … saying
e) … being looked at … becoming an …
f) … not being able to remember…
g) … coming back from …
h) Being deeply tanned … and wearing a colourful shirt …
i) Being very tired and ….
j) After waking up I saw my brother standing next to … and laughing
k) … leaving the reminder in its pocket.

| 40 – 32 Punkte | 31 – 20 Punkte | unter 20 Punkte |
|---|---|---|
| sehr gut bis gut | befriedigend bis ausreichend | nicht mehr ausreichend |

## Kapitel 6: *Infinitives:* Konstruktionen mit Infinitiv

### Aufgaben

Seite 52

1 to get; have been painted; be sung; to have bought; to be finding; be checked; to be put; to have been entered;

Seite 53

2 a) Mr Miller was the second to be bitten by the snake.
b) It is easy to see the difference between a poisonous snake and a slow worm.
c) Were they the only ones to take part in the pottery course?
d) She is certain to lose her job.

3 Yesterday my sister couldn't decide **whether to go to** to the cinema or **to meet** her friends. First, she wanted **to see** the new Harry Potter film, but she didn't know **how to get** into town. So she decided **to phone** her best friend but either of them was able to find out **where to watch** the film. My mother finally told them **where to go**. I really didn't know **whether to join** them or not.

Seite 54

4 a) … to be found … b) … to put his … c) … to be able to …

Seite 56

5 For a young person it is difficult to understand the advantages of a properly tidied room. Even for me it has never been easy to accept this. For my son it is terrible enough to sit in a clean room. He is always waiting for somebody to vacuum-clean his floor.

6 a) Peter wants his brother to read the letter aloud.
b) But he doesn't want the letter to be read by his parents.
c) That's why he expects his brother to hide the letter under his bed.

7 place to discover; so much to see; habitats to explore; let you enter; great to dive; to be seen; easy to touch; center to visit; visitors come; Let's enjoy; experience to choose; also get souvenirs; convince you **Seite 57**

## Training plus

34 *to-infinitive; bare infinitive* **Seite 58**

35 Nach **Adjektiven** und deren Steigerungsformen steht der ***to*-Infinitiv**.

36 to be read

37 I don't know who to phone.

38 Beispiellösung: somebody to talk to

39 a) Mein Bruder wollte seine Freundin verlassen.
b) Mein Bruder wollte, dass seine Freundin geht.
c) Mein Bruder veranlasste seine Freundin zu gehen.
d) Mein Bruder hatte seine Freundin verlassen.

40 in den Bedeutungen von *lassen, veranlassen, jdn. dazu bringen*; nach den modalen Hilfsverben mit Ausnahme von *ought to*; nach *had better, why not* und *would rather*

## Abschlusstest

1 a) The police made the thief open his bag. **Seite 59**
b) Robert ought to have breakfast at the moment.
c) Susan was wondering whether to read the newspaper or to watch TV.
d) He was the first man to land on the Moon.

2 a) … is the first to ask …
b) … ought to be brought back …
c) … a lot of work to do (to be done) …
d) … for her to smile …
e) … have …

3 a) It was the news about her father's death that made her fly to New York right away.
b) There her brother offered to let her stay in his house for a few days.
c) The funeral of a loved one is the most terrible thing to imagine.
d) Everybody expected her to hold a funeral ovation.
e) In church she didn't know whether to cry or to comfort her brother.
f) After three days in New York she was too exhausted to go back home immediately.

| 20 – 16 Punkte | 15 – 10 Punkte | unter 10 Punkte |
|---|---|---|
| sehr gut bis gut | befriedigend bis ausreichend | nicht mehr ausreichend |

# Kapitel 7: *Adverbs and adverbial phrases:* Adverbien und Adverbialsätze

## Aufgaben

**Seite 60** 1 nicely; new; happily; cautious; red; easily; slowly; careless; quickly; nervously; quickly; in an unfriendly way; nastily

**Seite 62** 2 pretty; pretty strange; nearly; calm; excited; simply; angrily; shrill; carefully; dead

**Seite 63** 3 a) Harry always meets Ron in the bookstore in London.
b) Today he goes into the magic shop with Hermione.
c) They want to buy a present for Ron at Abbot's.
d) Ron always gets ugly sweaters from his mum.
e) The Hogwarts Express leaves from platform 7 at eleven o'clock.

4 a) After Susan had left the house, Tom started to clean the kitchen.
b) She couldn't do it because she had sprained her ankle.
c) He wanted to help her because their holidays were coming nearer and nearer.
d) Although he had better things to do, he didn't stop until he was finished.
e) If she doesn't improve, we will have to cancel our trip to New York.

**Seite 64** 5 a) des Grundes b) der Zeit c) der Bedingung
d) der Einräumung e) des Ortes

**Seite 65** 6 a) Mike was late because he had overslept.
b) Although I didn't like her present, I thanked her.
c) I'll get up early on the day after the party so thet my parents won't see the mess.
d) I'll get myself a hamburger because I am hungry.

## Training plus

**Seite 65** 41 a) in and unfriendly way b) basically
c) hard/hardly d) quickly

42 a) He quickly left the room.
c) The driver stopped quickly **in front of the station at 11 o'clock**.

43 Wenn der Adverbialsatz vor dem Hauptsatz steht.

44 front position, mid position, end position

45 Ort vor Zeit

### Abschlusstest

1 0,5 Punkte pro richtige Lösung Seite 66
manner: silently, angrily, hard, fast, pretty, slowly, long, carefully, stupidly
place: at the end of the corridor, next to this old tower, into the house, behind the painting
time: in ancient times, lately, yesterday, for a few weeks, already
frequency: often
degree: hard, pretty, very,

2 0,5 Punkte pro richtige Lösung
deeply; nearly; Just; rather bad; lucky; far; slowly; politely; prettily; very angry; free; relentlessly; shocked; nice; quickly; lately; red; terrible; hardly; extremely bad; calm; smart; in an unfair way

3 a) Although I didn't like the food, I ate it.
b) After he had paid at the restaurant he forgot his wallet.
c) She started to cry because he had left her.
d) Before the young couple's car left the bride threw her flowers in the air.

| 34 – 27 Punkte | 26 – 17 Punkte | unter 17 Punkte |
|---|---|---|
| sehr gut bis gut | befriedigend bis ausreichend | nicht mehr ausreichend |

## Kapitel 8: *Conditional forms and sentences:* das Konditional und die Bedingungssätze

### Aufgaben

1 a) She wouldn't work on Sundays. Seite 68
b) The UN would never work against international cooperation.
c) UNICEF would like to narrow the gap between starvation and survival.
d) The organization would love to give children the right to grow up in health and peace.

2 a) I would accept the offer. Seite 69
b) Would you like to have a royal family in Germany?
c) Would you like to be rich or would you rather be happy?
d) Would he say that this candidate is best suited for this position?
e) I would rather think over it once again.

3 a) She would have been happy to meet Sir Peter Ustinov, a UNCEF Goodwill Ambassador.
b) The man who first climbed Mount Everest without artificial oxygen would have loved to meet Sir Edmund Hillary.
c) The winning basketball team would have loved to be invited by the host team after the match.
d) A great deal of famine in the world could have been eradicated.
e) Building a protective environment for our children should have been a main goal in our life.

4 a) If he is really interested in studying medicine, we won't stop him. Seite 70
b) If you want to buy this old horse, you will have to care for it.

c) If he does this, I'll leave him.
d) Even if what you say is true, I won't change my mind.
e) If we confirm this booking, we will travel to Norway this summer.

**Seite 71** 5 a) If she comes, I'll be happy.
b) If the US government introduces a new taxation, most Americans will support it.
c) If you google this word, you will get a lot of information about jazz.
d) If this quality newspaper shows too many photos, it will risk its reputation.

6 a) If she came, I would be happy.
b) If the US government introduced new taxation, most Americans would support it.
c) If you googled this word, you would get a lot of information about jazz.
d) If this quality newspaper showed too many photos, it would risk its reputation.

**Seite 72** 7 a) If the presidential candidate of the Democrats won this election, the Republicans would be extremely disappointed.
b) If you told him this secret, I would be rather angry.
c) If you used a different typeface, the layout of this page would be of higher quality.
d) If the International Court of Justice sentenced this war criminal, thousands of refugee victims would be satisfied.

8 a) If she had come, I would have been happy.
b) If the US government had introduced new taxation, most Americans would have supported it.
c) If you had googled this word, you would have got a lot of information about jazz.
d) If this quality newspaper had shown too many photos, it would have risked its reputation

9 a) If I had known this, I would never have agreed to it.
b) If you had been able to solve this problem, you would not have had to talk it over in the group once again.
c) If we had taken part in the bilingual lessons, we would have been able to translate this geographic text into English.
d) If I had entered the wrong PIN code another time, the money machine would have blocked my card.
e) If he had not had a character so charming, we would not have been cheated.
f) What would have happened, if she had missed the train?
g) If he had not told me stories about ship accidents all the time on the ferry to Hull, I would not have been in such a bad mood

**Seite 73** 10 a) If you write in smaller letters, you get more text on a page.
b) If we had taken the other path, we would sit/be sitting in the sun on the hotel terrace.
c) Whenever she comes, I'm pleased.

## Training plus

**Seite 74** 46 *Present Tense* im *if-clause*, *will-future* im Hauptsatz

47 *Past Tense* im *if-clause*, *Conditional I* im Hauptsatz

48 im *if-clause*

49 nein

50 HS: *Conditional II*; NS: *Past Perfect*

51 if

52 Typ III

53 Typ I

54 bei Allgemeingültigkeit

### Abschlusstest

Seite 75

1 a) If I had won the tennis match, I would have celebrated my victory.
b) Whenever I rub the plastic pole, there is electricity.
c) If they prolonged his contract, I would be extremely upset.
d) If you go on talking such nonsense about me, I will take the consequences.
e) If we had talked about the problems in time, we would not have to accept bankruptcy.
f) If you had posted the letter, we would have been able to book the journey.

2 a) Typ III b) Typ III c) Typ I d) Typ II
e) Typ II f) Typ III g) Typ II h) Typ I

3 a) entweder: If she ate …; oder: … she will become …;
b) If you had used …;
c) … we would live in a better world.
d) … if she wins this match.
e) … the apples come down.

| 25 – 20 Punkte | 19 – 13 Punkte | unter 13 Punkte |
| --- | --- | --- |
| sehr gut bis gut | befriedigend bis ausreichend | nicht mehr ausreichend |

## Kapitel 9: *Relative sentences:* Relativsätze

### Aufgaben

Seite 77

1 a) notwendig b) nicht notwendig c) notwendig
d) notwendig e) notwendig

2 a) Sally is talking to the girl who/that she argued with.
b) I love the Celtic song which/that I heard yesterday.
c) The old lady who/that lives in the house near the river has died.
d) The new TV spot which/that presents the XXL sports car is something which/that I don't like very much.

3 a) Robert is phoning the girl who addressed him on the playground some hours ago.
b) I think I know the film, the title of which I have forgotten.
c) Can you tell me the name of the young lady whose brother is practising with me in the judo club?

Seite 78

4 a) ☒ b) ☐ c) ☐

5 a) Eva is having an argument with the lady she talked to yesterday.

b) The document you filled in never came to me.
c) The book you are searching for is on my shelf.

**Seite 79** 6 a) My elder brother, who is an engineer, is constructing a model rocket.
b) The old house on the river, the name of which I think is Rio Caldo, is being sold.
c) The older sister of my aunt, whose younger brother has two sons, is my mother.
d) John, whose brother is 16, has been working at a garage for two years.

7 a) Rose, whose younger brother is often bullied at school, wants to talk to the headmaster.
b) My uncle's friend, who watched a James Bond movie yesterday, fainted this evening during dinner.
c) The cartoons in this magazine, which is sold in Germany and Austria, are terrible in my opinion.
d) The eight day outdoor camp, which was organized by students of our school, was a total success.
e) Paul, the 17-year-old boy from our neighbourhood, who was born in Atlanta, wants to get a college scholarship.

**Seite 80** 8 a) … which wasn't a bad idea.
b) … which, so I believe, was the best he could do.
c) … which really pleases me.

## Training plus

**Seite 80** 55 Nicht notwendige Relativsätze stehen immer zwischen Kommas.

56 Ein notwendiger Relativsatz, dessen Nebensatz zum Verständnis unverzichtbar ist.

57 *defining:* who, that, whose; *non-defining:* who, whose

58 Wenn das Relativpronomen das Objekt des Nebensatzes ist; nur in defining relative clauses!

## Abschlusstest

**Seite 81** 1 a) Sally, I'm really interested in the sightseeing tour I read about in the travel magazine.
b) Ken, where have you taken the horrible carpet I gave you as a Christmas present?
c) I don't like the way the problem is going to be solved.
d) More than 40 policemen were injured in the riots that started on Monday.
e) I'm worried about the fact that several persons have become infected by bird flu.

2 a) I talked to the old lady ~~that~~/~~who~~/whose/~~which~~ car had broken down in front of the church.
b) Mrs. Dexter did not see the snake which/that/~~who~~/~~whose~~ was approaching on the floor.
c) Sydney, ~~that~~/~~who~~/~~whose~~/which is the largest city in Australia, is not the capital.
d) The World Wide Web, ~~that~~/~~who~~/~~whose~~/which was invented by a US-American, has changed our life.
e) They're planning to build a new activity park down by the river, ~~that~~/~~who~~/which I think is a great idea.

3 a) I love the Italian food that/which is served in the pizzeria at the corner.
b) He will make an offer we won't be able to accept.
c) A giraffe is an animal living/that lives/which lives in the savanna.

| 26 – 21 Punkte | 20 – 13 Punkte | unter 13 Punkte |
|---|---|---|
| sehr gut bis gut | befriedigend bis ausreichend | nicht mehr ausreichend |

## Kapitel 10: *Reported Speech:* Indirekte Rede

1 a) He says that his parents mustn't know about this. Seite 82
b) He says he doesn't know how to solve this problem.
c) He says the only thing he can do is repair it.

2 a) He said his parents mustn't know about that. Seite 84
b) He said he didn't know how to solve that problem.
c) He said the only thing he could do was repair it.

3 a) He says he can see nothing with these glasses.
b) He reported that she hadn't been allowed to see him.
c) She said that that couldn't be possible.
d) He said that he had to tell me the truth.

4 Beispiellösung Seite 85
After I had been waiting for an hour I asked Jay if he was going to come. I told him that we wanted to be at the party 30 minutes before and that I had been waiting there for nearly one hour. Jay asked me if I couldn't be a little more patient. He claimed that he had had to wash his hair and that he still didn't know what trousers he would wear. He told me that I hadn't really been much help. I answered that I simply couldn't understand it. I said that he had been putting on trousers and T-shirts endlessly. I asked him who he wanted to impress. Jay answered that it was not a matter of impressing somebody, but a matter of style. I told him that the last person I had waited for so long was my ex-girlfriend. I told him that he was even slower than her. I added that he was a boy and asked him if he was finally finished. Jay answered that he couldn't go, because he still had to dry his hair. I responded that I was leaving.

5 One of the tourists asked if Ford had invented/invented the car. Another visitor asked how expensive cars had been compared to today. Someone else asked asked how that could be/could have been achieved. A woman asked if he had invented/invented new methods of production. Somebody else asked how much time they had saved/saved by that method. Another tourist asked if other car manufacturers had reacted/reacted. Someone asked why that had been - was so important. He added that cars weren't/aren't really that necessary. Finally, somebody asked if high pollution and the destruction of our environment aren't also results of his changes. Seite 86

6 a) I wanted to know how long he had been living in that street. Seite 88
b) He told me that he had been living there since he was born.
c) My mother asked him if he did any sports.
d) Chris said that he had been playing soccer for 10 years then and that he had won the city competition twice.

e) Then my father advised him not to eat too much before a game, because otherwise he wouldn't be able to run fast.
f) I told my father not to meddle with other people's business.
g) Then Chris asked if we had already had lunch. He invited us to a barbecue with his family.

## Training plus

Seite 89

59 *timeshift*

60 command/order/tell s.b. to do s.th.

61 ... sich Zeit oder Ort, an dem etwas gesagt wird, auch ändern.

62 ... dass Angaben in der direkten Rede in der indirekten Rede in eine ‚tiefere' Vergangenheitsstufe gesetzt werden.

63 the day before

64 Beispiellösung: invite/offer/ask (s.b.)

65 suggest doing s.th. odder suggest that s.th. should be done

## Abschlusstest

Seite 90

1 Gehe von maximal 30 Bewertungseinheiten aus und ziehe pro Fehler eine Bewertungseinheit ab.
First of all, I congratulated Mike on his fantastic new record. I asked him how he felt. He answered that they were still pretty much exhausted and that he couldn't believe they had really won the award. I asked if they were going to celebrate that night. He said they were and added that he thought they would have some of their crew and the managers over for a little party. I told Ouzo that his guitar work seemed to have improved very much and asked him what he had done to become so good. Ouzo replied that he had done nothing. He explained that they had never had so much time to produce their album. Their manager had cancelled nearly all the gigs up to then and so the band had been able to concentrate on every little detail. Then he asked me to excuse him for a moment because he had to go to the bathroom. I said to Mike that he/Ouzo seemed to be a bit nervous. I wanted to know if the rumours were true that he had started taking hard drugs again, since his girlfriend Amy had left him. Mike asked me not to ask any questions about drugs. He claimed that their band was clean. But I said that he had to admit that drugs were/are a great problem for a lot of musicians. Mike told me that he was fed up with those questions. Then I asked what their plans would be for the rest of the season. He responded that they were going to play a few concerts in America and Japan. He added that it wouldn't be a big tour. He explained that after the tour they would have their well-deserved holiday before they prepared their world tour in October. I then asked him to sign a T-shirt for us. I told him that our magazine was collecting autographs from all the stars we could get hold of. I claimed that we were/are planning to offer the T-shirt at a charity auction which will be held next September. I added that we hoped/hope to get a good price for it since it was/is a good cause. Mike asked what kind of cause it was/is for. I answered that we wanted/want to build a school in Afghanistan. Mike said that he would support that idea. I finally thanked him for the interview.

2 Setze je zwei Bewertungseinheiten für jeden richtigen Satz ein.
**Man:** "I can't see properly, because the man in front of me is so tall. My back is aching since my seat is not comfortable enough. When is the break? I'm thirsty!"
**Woman:** "Stop snoring!"
**Man:** "I've never seen such a lousy play. Why are the people behind us constantly shushing?"
**Woman:** "Would you please be quiet! Either close your eyes and go to sleep or just sit and watch!"

| 46 – 37 Punkte | 36 – 23 Punkte | unter 23 Punkte |
|---|---|---|
| sehr gut bis gut | befriedigend bis ausreichend | nicht mehr ausreichend |

## Kapitel 11: *Comment and Composition*

### Aufgaben

1 Beispiellösung: Seite 92
**Intro:** new research: kids spend to much time in front of the screen; heated controversy …
**Main body:**
**Pros:** quick access to information, getting into contact with other people in chatrooms, via skype, the Internet as a business platform, „gaming"
**Cons:** risk of addiction, lack of personal contacts, abuse of private data
**Conclusion:** favouring/not favouring the statement, reasons, arguments

2 Beispiellösung: Seite 94
a) Since ancient Greek times wisdom has been an elementary topic in philosophical discussions.
b) Since their introduction in so many schools around the world, school uniforms have both been welcomed and abhorred.
c) Apart from being a medical term, addiction in any form has been present in any era and at any time.
d) For some, tradition may seem to be an archaic word, for others it is the bridging link to virtue.

3 a) For these reasons we might claim that … Seite 95
b) In spite of this development …
c) This topic has often been discussed

### Training plus

66 title - introduction - main body (pros and cons) - conclusion and final statement Seite 96

67 nach Möglichkeit mindestens drei (pro pros und cons)

68 pros und cons

69 a) Firstly …, Secondly, …, Thirdly …, Last but not least …
b) On the one hand …, On the other hand …
c) To begin with …, Then …, Moreover, …, Last but not least …

70 a) Yet/Still … b) Contrary to …
c) In spite of this …

71 eventuell in der Schlussbemerkung

72 Beispiellösung: Many parents claim that advertising at school might result in a permanent competition among pupils who have to decide whether to go along with fashionable trends or swim against the mass.

73 For all these reasons …

74 On the one hand …, on the other hand …;

### Abschlusstest

Freie Schülerlösung. Am besten bittest du deine Lehrkraft, deine Arbeit durchzusehen.

| 30 – 24 Punkte | 23 – 15 Punkte | unter 15 Punkte |
|---|---|---|
| sehr gut bis gut | befriedigend bis ausreichend | nicht mehr ausreichend |

## Kapitel 12: *Cartoons:* Karikaturen

### Aufgaben

Seite 98

1 Beispiellösung:
A man on a tree is sawing the branch he is sitting on. So he will fall down in a few minutes as a result of his silly action.

2 Beispiellösung:
The cartoon verbalizes the problem of gaining firewood in arid regions thus illustrating the fact that even the smallest potential of resources in developing countries often have to be sacrificed in order to secure people's basic needs.

3 Freie Schülerlösung
Am besten bittest du deine Lehrkraft, die Ausarbeitung des Cartoons zu korrigieren.

### Training plus

Seite 100

75 Beschreibung der Situation – Darstellung der Botschaft – Interpretation

76 cartoonist

77 speech bubble, thought bubble

78 caption

79 facial expression, posture

80 The cartoonist refers to the problem of mass unemployment.

## Abschlusstest

Seite 101

Freie Schülerlösung
Am besten bittest du deine Lehrkraft, die Interpretation zu korrigieren.

| 20 – 16 Punkte | 15 – 10 Punkte | unter 10 Punkte |
|---|---|---|
| sehr gut bis gut | befriedigend bis ausreichend | nicht mehr ausreichend |

# Kapitel 13: Texte zusammenfassen und Mediation

## Aufgaben

Seite 102

1 Wichtig: c, d, e, g, h, i, j, k, m, n
Unwichtig: a, b, f, l

Seite 104

2 a) furniture b) religions c) stars/celebrities
d) American presidents e) professions

3 a) Starting their German Tour in Munich last night, Metallica was working solidly through their repertoire.
b) Being problably the most democratic band, they were playing on a 360° stage positioned in the centre of the arena.
c) After publishing Death Magnetic in 2008 Metallica has been everybody's darling.
d) The stadium actually being too small, many people were waiting outside.

Seite 105

4 a) ("I was Kaiser Bill's batman", was Whistling Jack Smith's hit in the 60s, the Scorpions whistled "Winds of Change" in the 90s); (The happy-go-lucky song … at the zoo.)
b) Beispiellösung:
Ujian, a 10-year-old Orang Utan of the Heidelberg Zoo, is able to whistle melodies almost perfectly. In June a Tobias Kämmerer production starring Ujian (entitled "Ich bin Ujian") will be released. There will be five different versions on the CD.

## Training plus

Seite 107

81 Present tense

82 indirekte Rede *(reported speech)*

83 Both the cost of shipping and that of chartering ships have greatly decreased.

84 Herausfinden der Hauptgedanken

85 schnelles Lesen, um wichtige Teilaspekte herauszufiltern

86 das sinngemäße Übertragen aus der Originalsprache

87 den Texttyp

88 übergeordnete Begriffe, Nebensatzverkürzung, Verrkürzung von Teilsätzen mit Infinitiven

89 I'd like to discuss the greenhouse effect.

90 Let me express my deepest/strongest disapproval concerning your article published in your newspaper yesterday.

## Abschlusstest

**Seite 109**

1 Beispiellösung
Zeilen 1 - 8: Examples of bullying
Zeilen 9 - 12: Bullying and the digital age
Zeilen13 - 17: Bullying and anonymity
Zeilen 18 - 22: Just a click
Zeilen 23 - 37: Global bullying

2 Freie Schülerlösung
Am besten du bittest einen Mitschüler oder deine Lehrkraft die Zusammenfassung zu überprüfen.

3 Freie Schülerlösung
Am besten du bittest einen Mitschüler oder deine Lehrkraft die Zusammenfassung zu überprüfen.

4 Er wurde zuvor von drei Ärzten getestet und als ein überdurchschnittliches menschliches Wesen befunden. In der ersten Woche nahm er 10 Pfund zu. Einen Monat später hatte er insgesamt 25 Pfund zugelegt. Sein Cholesterinspiegel war um 65 Punkte angestiegen (ein Drittel höher als zuvor). Am schockierendsten war jedoch folgendes: Sein Arzt, der den Filmemacher gebeten hatte, das Experiment nach drei Wochen zu beenden, nahm an, dass das permanente Essen von Fast Food einen ernsthaften Leberschaden hervorrief, ähnlich jenem, den Nicolas Cage in seiner Filmrolle in Leaving Las Vegas erfährt. Im Abspann des Filmes hält Spurlock fest, dass er 14 Monate brauchte, um seinen früheren körperlichen Zustand wieder herzustellen.
Spurlocks Film ist viel mehr als ein medizinisches Journal. Spurlock verbindet Leinwandpräsenz mit einer feine Prise Eigenmissbilligung und perfektem Timing bezüglich der komischen Elemente. In einer Szene wird er dabei gefilmt, wie er sein erstes Supper Size Meal vorne in seinem Auto isst. Diese Szene beginnt damit, wie er voller Freude über die riesenhaften Portionen die Hände reibt … und endet damit, wie er sich am Autofenster übergibt.

| 65 - 52 Punkte | 51 - 33 Punkte | unter 33 Punkte |
|---|---|---|
| sehr gut bis gut | befriedigend bis ausreichend | nicht mehr ausreichend |

## Kapitel 14: Sich zu Filmen äußern

### Aufgaben

1 a) close-up b) long shot c) full shot **Seite 110**

2 a) Diese faszinierende Szene zeigt ein Augenpaar während eines Duells in einer Close-up-Einstellung.
b) Vielleicht erkennen Sie zwei Personen in Rettungswesten in einer Full-shot-Einstellung.
c) Diese Totaleinstellung ermöglicht es dem Betrachter eine wunderbare Seenlandschaft zu überblicken.

3 In this scene Charlie Chaplin is viewed from above. Such an angle is called an aerial shot. This way he appears even more ridiculous. Later in the film he is shown in a tracking shot sitting in a driving car. **Seite 111**

### Training plus

91 Kameraperspektive und Kamerabewegung werden im Englischen **camera angle** und **camera movement** genannt. **Seite 114**

92 Zooming in bedeutet, dass **das gefilmte Objekt mithilfe der Objektivtechnik optisch herangezogen wird.**

93 **flashback**

94 **flash forward, foreshadowing**

95 **director**

96 shot sequence

97 back lighting

98 character

99 fade in

### Abschlusstest

Freie Schülerlösung: Am besten du bittest deine Lehrkraft deine Szenenbeschreibung durchzusehen. **Seite 115**

| 30 – 24 Punkte | 23 – 15 Punkte | unter 15 Punkte |
|---|---|---|
| sehr gut bis gut | befriedigend bis ausreichend | nicht mehr ausreichend |

# Verbtabelle

Diese Liste wichtiger unregelmäßiger Verben enthält neben Infinitiv und *simple past*-Form auch die dritte Form, nämlich die des Perfekts (z.B. *to go - went - gone*; gehen - ging - gegangen).

| infinitive | simple past | perfect | deutsch |
|---|---|---|---|
| to be | was/were | been | sein |
| to beat | beat | beaten | schlagen, besiegen |
| to bring | brought | brought | bringen |
| to buy | bought | bought | kaufen |
| to choose | chose | chosen | wählen, aussuchen |
| to cling | clung | clung | festhalten, sich klammern |
| to come | came | come | kommen |
| to do | did | done | machen, tun |
| to draw | drew | drawn | zeichnen |
| to dream | dreamt | dreamt | träumen |
| to drink | drank | drunk | trinken |
| to drive | drove | driven | fahren |
| to eat | ate | eaten | essen |
| to fall | fell | fallen | fallen |
| to feed | fed | fed | füttern |
| to feel | felt | felt | (sich) fühlen |
| to fight | fought | fought | kämpfen, streiten |
| to find | found | found | finden |
| to fly | flew | flown | fliegen |
| to forget | forgot | forgot/forgotten | vergessen |
| to get | got | got/gotten | bekommen |
| to give | gave | given | geben |
| to go | went | gone | gehen |
| to grow | grew | grown | wachsen, anbauen |
| to have | had | had | haben |
| to hear | heard | heard | hören |
| to hit | hit | hit | treffen, schlagen |
| to hurt | hurt | hurt | weh tun, verletzen |
| to know | knew | known | kennen, wissen |
| to learn | learnt | learnt | lernen |

| infinitive | simple past | perfect | deutsch |
|---|---|---|---|
| to let | let | let | lassen |
| to lie | lay | lain | liegen |
| to lose | lost | lost | verlieren |
| to make | made | made | machen, tun |
| to mean | meant | meant | bedeuten |
| to meet | met | met | (sich) treffen |
| to put | put | put | setzen, stellen, legen |
| to read | read | read | lesen |
| to ride | rode | ridden | reiten, fahren |
| to run | ran | run | laufen, rennen |
| to say | said | said | sagen |
| to see | saw | seen | sehen |
| to send | sent | sent | schicken, senden |
| to set | set | set | setzen, stellen, legen |
| to shake | shook | shaken | schütteln |
| to shine | shined/shone | shined/shone | scheinen, glänzen |
| to shut | shut | shut | schließen, zumachen |
| to sing | sang | sung | singen |
| to sit | sat | sat | sitzen |
| to sleep | slept | slept | schlafen |
| to speak | spoke | spoken | sprechen |
| to spell | spelt | spelt | buchstabieren |
| to spend | spent | spent | verbringen, ausgeben |
| to stand | stood | stood | stehen |
| to swim | swam | swum | schwimmen |
| to take | took | taken | nehmen |
| to teach | taught | taught | lehren, unterrichten |
| to tell | told | told | sagen, erzählen |
| to think | thought | thought | denken, meinen |
| to throw | threw | thrown | werfen |
| to understand | understood | understood | verstehen |
| to wake | waked/woke | waked/woken | wecken |
| to wear | wore | worn | tragen |
| to win | won | won | siegen, gewinnen |
| to write | wrote | written | schreiben |

# Glossar

### Adjektiv *(adjective)*
Gibt Auskunft darüber, wie etwas ist (Wiewort); steht vor → Nomen oder im Zusammenhang mit dem → Verb ***to be***. Beispiel: ***the nice boy; the boy is nice.***

### Adverb *(adverb)*
Umstandswort. Gibt an, wie, wo, wie oft oder zu welcher Zeit man etwas tut. Beispiel: ***happily, angrily; often, always, today, yesterday; here, there; ...a***

### Adverbiale Bestimmung
Umstandsbestimmung. Gibt an, wie, wo, wie oft oder zu welcher Zeit man etwas tut. Beispiel: ***the right way, in angry tones; under the car, behind the curtain; once a week, from time to time; on Monday, in 1998***

### Aktiv *(active clause)*
Wenn das Subjekt des Satzes handelt, steht das Verb in der Aktiv-Form. Beispiel: ***I read this book. – Ich lese dieses Buch.*** Das Gegenteil ist das → Passiv.

### Artikel, unbestimmter *(indefinite article)*
Beschreibt eine nicht näher bestimmte Person oder Sache. Beispiel: ***an apple; a green apple – ein Apfel; ein grüner Apfel.***

### Bedingungssatz *(if-clause, conditional sentence)*
Drückt aus, dass etwas unter einer bestimmten Bedingung geschieht. Bedingungssätze des Typs 1 beschreiben erfüllbare Bedingungen. Beispiel: ***If I clean my room, mum will be very happy.***

### *conditional sentence*
→ Bedingungssatz

### Demonstrativpronomen *(demonstrative pronoun)*
Wortart, mit deren Hilfe der Sprecher/die Sprecherin auf einen Gesprächsgegenstand verweist, auf den man z. B. mit dem Finger zeigen kann. Beispiel ***this*** (→ Singular), ***these*** (→ Plural); ***that*** (→ Singular), ***those*** (→ Plural).

### *gerund*
Verb in der *-ing*-Form, das die Funktion eines Substantivs hat. Beispiel: ***I like reading. – Ich mag (das) Lesen.***

### *going to-future*
Drückt aus, dass jemand etwas plant oder triftige Gründe oder Anzeichen dafür sprechen, dass etwas eintritt. Beispiel: ***I am going to fly to Rio next week.***

### Grundform *(infinitive)*
Infinitiv des → Verbs ohne Hinweise auf Personen oder Zeitform (Tempus). Beispiel: ***drive, eat, drink ...***

### Hilfsverb, modales *(modal auxiliary verb)*
Kann nur in Verbindung mit einem → Vollverb das → Prädikat eines Satzes bilden. Beispiel: ***I must help my father this afternoon. Jenny can play football!***

### *if-clause*
→ Bedingungssatz

### Indirekte Rede *(reported speech)*
Gibt wieder, was jemand gesagt hat. Gegensatz zur direkten Rede. Besteht aus dem Redebegleitsatz ***(reporting clause)*** und der wiedergegebenen Aussage ***(reported clause)***. Beispiel: ***She says (reporting clause) that her teacher is ill (reported clause).***

**Infinitiv *(infinitive)***
→ Grundform des → Verbs.

**Konsonant *(consonant)***
Mitlaut. Beispiel *[p, t, k]*. Das Gegenteil ist der → Vokal (Selbstlaut).

***Mediation***
Sinngemäße Übersetzung mit Umschreibung. Das Gegenteil ist die wortwörtliche Übersetzung *(translation)*.

**Modales Hilfsverb *(modal auxiliary verb)***
→ Hilfsverb, modales

**Passiv *(passive clause)***
Das Subjekt eines Satzes handelt nicht selbst, sondern etwas wird mit ihm gemacht bzw. es „erleidet" eine Handlung. Das Verb steht dann in der Passiv-Form. Beispiel: ***The car was stolen.*** – **Das Auto wurde gestohlen.** Das Gegenteil ist das → Aktiv.

***past perfect progressive* (Verlaufsform des Plusquamperfekts)**
Drückt aus, dass eine Handlung vor einer anderen Handlung in der Vergangenheit ablief. Die Betonung liegt auf dem Verlauf der Handlung und nicht auf deren Ergebnis. Beispiel: ***He had been walking for several hours when he arrived at the cabin.***

***past perfect (simple)***
Das ***past perfect simple*** entspricht im Wesentlichen dem deutschen Plusquamperfekt. Es ist eine Zeitform der Vergangenheit, die zum Ausdruck der Vorvergangenheit benötigt wird. Beispiel: ***I had lived in this house.***

***past progressive* (Verlaufsform der Vergangenheit)**
Drückt aus, das eine Handlung in der Vergangenheit gerade ablief oder dass es sich um eine Hintergrundhandlung handelt. Beispiel: ***She was preparing dinner when the door bell rang.***

**Plural *(plural)***
Mehrzahl. Beispiel: ***flowers, stones …***

**Prädikat *(predicate)***
Satzaussage; besteht aus einem → Vollverb oder aus einem Vollverb und einem Hilfsverb. Beispiel: ***He likes pizza. She must play the trumpet.***

**Präposition *(preposition)***
Verhältniswort; drückt im Satz das Verhältnis von Personen und Dingen zueinander aus. Es gibt z. B. Präpositionen des Ortes, der Richtung oder der Zeit.

***present perfect (simple)***
Form der Vergangenheit, die angibt, dass in der Vergangenheit etwas gerade geschehen ist. Drückt aus, dass beendete Handlungen/ Ereignisse Auswirkungen auf die Gegenwart haben. Beispiel: ***She has phoned her husband. (They want to take the train together.)***

***present perfect progressive* (Verlaufsform des Perfekt)**
Wenn die Voraussetzungen für das *present perfect* gegeben sind, aber der Verlauf betont werden soll, wird das *present perfect progressive* verwendet. Ein wichtiges Signalwort ist *just* (= gerade eben). Beispiel: ***I have (just) been wondering what you asked me.***

***present progressive* (Verlaufsform der Gegenwart)**
Drückt aus, was im Moment des Sprechens passiert bzw. was jemand im Moment des Sprechens tut. Beispiel: ***It is raining at the moment. Susi and Pete are playing football.*** Signalwörter für das *present progressive* sind zum Beispiel ***at the moment, now.***

### Pronomen *(pronouns)*
Wörter, die für (lateinisch: pro) ein Nomen stehen. Durch sie vermeidet man z. B die Wiederholung eines Nomens. Es gibt z. B. → Personalpronomen oder → Reflexivpronomen.

### Reflexivpronomen *(reflexive pronouns)*
Beziehen sich auf ein vorher genanntes Nomen. Beispiel: ***myself, yourself, herself, himself, itself*** (→ Singular); ***ourselves, yourselves, themselves*** (→ Plural).

### Relativpronomen
Fürwort, das auf das Nomen des Hauptsatzes verweist. Relativpronomen können Subjekt oder Objekt des Nebensatzes sein. Beispiel: *Tom is a boy who loves sports.* Relativpronomen sind z. B. *who, that, which.*

### Relativsatz
Nebensatz, der sich auf das Nomen des Hauptsatzes bezieht. Beispiel: *The book which/that I'm reading is very interesting.*

### Satz
Ein vollständiger Aussagesatz besteht mindestens aus einem Subjekt und einem Prädikat. Die Satzstellung *(word order)* im englischen Aussagesatz folgt dem Muster Subjekt - Verb/Prädikat - Objekt bzw. *subject - verb/predicate - object (S - P - O).*

### Satzglied
Teil des Satzes. Besteht aus einem Wort oder einer Wortgruppe. Beispiel: *My dog/ hates/black cats.* Die bekanntesten Satzglieder sind → Subjekt (*subject*), → Prädikat (*predicate*) und → Objekt (*object*).

### *simple past* (einfache Vergangenheit)
Gibt in der Vergangenheit abgeschlossene Handlungen wider. Beispiel: *I watched TV last night.* Signalwörter für das *simple past* sind zum Beispiel: *last week, yesterday, three years ago.*

### *simple present* (einfache Gegenwartsform)
Wird verwendet, wenn etwas immer wieder so passiert oder immer wieder so ist. Beispiel: *We always have breakfast in the kitchen. Every morning, he gets up late.* Signalwörter für das *simple present* sind zum Beispiel ***always, every, usually.***

### Singular *(singular)*
Einzahl. Beispiel: *flower, stone ...*

### Subjekt *(subject)*
Satzgegenstand; Satzglied im 1. Fall bzw. Nominativ; Frage: Wer?/Was? Beispiel: *The teacher sounds angry.*

### Verb *(verb)*
Tätigkeitswort oder Zeitwort. Beispiel: *walk, he talked, he has lost.*

### Verb, unregelmäßig *(verb, irregular)*
Bildet die Vergangenheitsformen unregelmäßig. Beispiel: *drive - drove - driven; go - went - gone.*

### Vollverb *(main verb)*
Kann allein das → Prädikat eines Satzes bilden, d. h. ohne ein → Hilfsverb. Beispiel: *Elephants eat a lot!*

### *will-future*
Drückt Vorhersagen oder Vermutungen über die Zukunft aus, die nicht beeinflussbar sind oder verweist auf spontane Entschlüsse. Beispiel: *It will be cloudy tomorrow. Wait, I will help you!*

### Zeit *(time)*/Zeitform *(tenses)*
Zeit lässt sich in die Bereiche Vergangenheit, Gegenwart und Zukunft aufteilen. Zeit wird durch die Zeitformen *(tenses)* ausgedrückt. Beispiel: *present tense: simple present* und *present progressive; past tense: simple past* und *past perfect; future: will-future* und *going to-future.*

# Stichwortverzeichnis

## M



## N



## P



## R



## S



## T



## V



## W



## Z